MW01670591

DAG HEWARD-MILLS

# *The* ART *of the* FOLLOWER

*Using the Lessons of Jesus to Become the Follower God Wants Us to Be*

Carpenter's Son Publishing

The Art of the Follower: Using the Lessons of Jesus to Become the Follower God Wants Us to Be

Copyright © 2013 by Dag Heward-Mills

All rights reserved. No part of this book may be reproduced or transmitted in any form or by any means, electronic or mechanical, including photocopying, recording or by any information storage and retrieval system, without permission in writing from the copyright owner.

Unless otherwise noted, Scripture references are taken from *The Holy Bible: King James Version.*

Published by Carpenter's Son Publishing, Franklin, Tennessee

Published in association with Larry Carpenter of Christian Book Services, LLC
www.christianbookservices.com

Edited by Paul Lewis

Cover and Interior Layout Design by Suzanne Lawing

Printed in the United States of America

978-0-9883962-7-2

# Table of Contents

**Part I: Following Is Eternally Significant . . . . . . . . . . . . . 5**

Chapter 1: What Is the Art of Following? . . . . . . . . . . . . . . 9

Chapter 2: How to Succeed at Following. . . . . . . . . . . . . . 13

Chapter 3: Seven Ways to Practice Following . . . . . . . . . . 21

Chapter 4: What Jesus Taught About Following . . . . . . . . 25

Chapter 5: The Art of Not Following . . . . . . . . . . . . . . . . 31

**Part II: Following God's Champions . . . . . . . . . . . . . . . 37**

Chapter 6: The Art of Following Abraham . . . . . . . . . . . . 39

Chapter 7: The Art of Following Isaac. . . . . . . . . . . . . . . . 57

Chapter 8: The Art of Following Jacob . . . . . . . . . . . . . . . 69

Chapter 9: The Art of Following Joseph . . . . . . . . . . . . . . 81

Chapter 10: The Art of Following Moses. . . . . . . . . . . . . . 97

Chapter 11: The Art of Following Joshua . . . . . . . . . . . . 103

Chapter 12: The Art of Following David. . . . . . . . . . . . . . 111

Chapter 13: The Art of Following Solomon. . . . . . . . . . . 131

Chapter 14: The Art of Following Nehemiah . . . . . . . . . 143

Chapter 15: The Art of Following Esther. . . . . . . . . . . . . 153

Chapter 16: The Art of Following Daniel . . . . . . . . . . . . 167

**Part III: Following Begins At Home . . . . . . . . . . . . . . . 179**

Chapter 17: Like Father, Like Son. . . . . . . . . . . . . . . . . . 181

Chapter 18: True Sons and Their Rewards. . . . . . . . . . . . 197

# PART I

# Following is Eternally Significant

FOLLOWING!

At first glance the practice appears innocent and simple enough . . . safe . . . and usually rewarding. But, beware my friend! Following is actually a very powerful practice . . . frequently risky . . . sometimes life-threatening . . . and always consequential.

In everyday language we often hear and speak about following. Notice these common expressions:

Follow the leader
You're following too close
Just follow me!
Don't follow me. I'm lost too! (bumper sticker)
Follow your nose
She/he has quite a following
Follow the money
Follow directions
I think I'm being followed
I was just following orders

Follow-up
Follow-through

So, who are you following? I don't mean breaking news, a favourite performer or sports team. I'm asking about the beliefs you follow -- the ones that shape your personal values and attitudes. What defines the true significance of your life? Who do you look to for guidance? Which teacher has the answers that satisfy your soul? Whether intentionally or unknowingly, everyone is following someone.

If we're truthful, the first answer is usually "me." I follow me! Indeed, every one of us begins in life following ourselves, our own wants, our desires, our personal passions. Eventually, most of us also notice the value in altruistic efforts that bless others. But, truth be told, without the "feel good" rewards of these activities, we eventually struggle to sustain them. For, at our core we are all sons of Adam and products of "the Fall." Our carnal hearts march to the drumbeat of "self" -- alienated from the Maker who created us to know and enjoy an intimate and personal relationship with Him. It is our untamed "me" -- our selfish rebellion -- that bars us from this righteous pleasure.

Paul declares in Romans 3:10, "There is none righteous, no not one." The prophet Isaiah penned, "All we like sheep have gone astray, we have turned everyone to his own way" (Isaiah 53:6). Fortunately, he prophetically adds the solution: "but the Lord has laid on him the iniquity of us all." Jesus said of himself in Matthew 20:28, "Just as the Son of Man did not come to be served, but to serve, and to give his life as a ransom for many." You may have recited from your childhood the familiar words of John 3:16: "For God so loved the world, that he gave his only begotten Son, that whosoever believes in him should not perish, but have everlasting life."

This promise of salvation -- the redemption opportunity each of us needs so badly -- was fulfilled in the life and death of our Saviour, the Lord Jesus Christ. This salvation gift from God himself becomes real for you when you receive it. "He made Him who knew no sin to be sin on our behalf, so that we might become the righteousness of God in Him" (2 Corinthians 5:21).

Salvation cannot be acquired by working diligently to imitate Christ. Ephesians 2:8-10 instructs us, "For it is by grace [unmerited favor] you have been saved, through faith -- and this not from yourselves, it is the gift of God -- not by works so that no one can boast. For we are God's workmanship, created in Christ Jesus to do good works, which God prepared in advance for us to do." When correctly understood, this amazing redemption and new standing with God daily motivates our love and obedience to Jesus Christ.

The true Christian believer "follows" Jesus Christ. And following him is serious business -- a life-long commitment to being his disciple as a mature follower. Some twenty centuries ago, Simon called Peter and his brother Andrew were the first to hear and respond when Jesus said, "Come, follow me . . ." (Matthew 4:19).

Since that day, thousands of millions have followed their example -- heeding Christ's eternity-changing invitation to "Follow Me!" Jesus is the only worthy one to follow because he is the Christ, the only begotten of the Father and the only Saviour of all mankind.

Over the next five chapters, I pray your mind will be illuminated and your heart will thrill to a deeper understanding of the Art of the Follower.

CHAPTER 1

# What Is The Art of Following?

Throughout your Christian journey, many leaders will request your allegiance. Always the first question you must ask is, "But, who are you following?" If, upon examination, that leader's life validates that he or she is truly following Jesus, then you may follow safely. However, one must never lose sight of the truth that only Jesus Christ can forgive your sins and one-day present you faultless before the Father. So, first and always, follow Jesus!

## Defining The Art Of Following

- The art of following is the art of copying
- The art of emulating someone
- The art of imitating something
- The art of trying to be like someone
- The art of reproduction
- The art of cloning
- The art of becoming a double
- The art of becoming a twin

- The art of catching up
- The art of surging forward

## Success Follows Following

Children naturally and instinctively employ the art of following. By copying, children surge forward with leaps and bounds -- learning to speak complex languages in very short periods of time. Following, copying or emulating accomplishes almost all the learning younger children do.

Following, however, isn't just a personal practice of individuals. Many nations -- rich for centuries -- became so by following. Europe and America largely used the art of following to become among the oldest and most prosperous nations in the world. Through emulation, each European country became like their neighbours and developed into an almost identical wealthy state. Their roads, buildings, and other infrastructures are similar. Their banking and economic systems are almost identical. Their military capabilities match. The lifestyles of the people and the conditions of living are similar in each of these countries. Indeed, through emulation, the nations caught up with neighbours -- refusing to be left behind in the race for prosperity.

Similarly, nations more recently rich also employed following. Taiwan, China, and Korea are well known for their ability to follow and copy. Indeed, most nations that have become wealthy in the last fifty years are masters at the art of following. These wealthy nations are well known for their ability to copy. Indeed, many of their products are clearly imitations. They produced cars that were virtually exact replicas of well-known European models. The Koreans are not embarrassed by modelling their Daewoo cars after Opel, and the Ssangyong after Mercedes Benz and the Hyundai after Toyota. Through their shameless copying, they quickly caught up and surged forward to become leading carmakers.

In almost every field of technology and endeavour, they have caught up and surged forward, creating wealth that others could only dream of. Those who were ashamed to copy could only stand by as the masters of copying surged ahead to become millionaires and billionaires.

Jesus Christ, the Son of God, Used the Art of Following

Jesus, too, used the art of following to transform illiterate fishermen into leaders and managers of a worldwide movement. If the Son of God would use the art of following as His method of training, it must be the highest and most superior method of learning, training and teaching.

The art of following is the art of imitating and copying someone. The art of following is the art of becoming like the person you admire. The art of following is the art of becoming a replica of a person that is ahead of you. Through the careful and thoughtful use of the art of following, you will be able to catch up and surge forward in your life and your ministry. Even more importantly, you will become a wiser, more mature, more passionate, and more effective disciple of the Lord Jesus Christ.

# CHAPTER 2

# How To Succeed at Following

*That ye be not slothful, but followers ...* HEBREWS 6:12

There are many commands in the Scriptures that instruct believers to follow people. The Bible is replete with instructive examples. So let's take a careful look at nine guiding principles that will guide your success at following, copying, emulating and catching up with those ahead of you in the faith.

## Nine Principles of Following

**1. You succeed at the art of following by first choosing to follow God Himself.**

> *BE YE therefore FOLLOWERS OF GOD as dear children AND WALK IN LOVE, as Christ also hath loved us and hath given himself for us an offering and a sacrifice to God for a sweet smelling savour.* 1 CORINTHIANS 5:1-2

Successfully following God involves daily walking in love and sacrifice.

Have you realised that it is possible to follow God? Which better Person is there to follow than God? The Word of God shows us exactly what to do if we want to follow Him. All we must do is learn how to love and how to sacrifice. Faithfully doing these two things will ensure that you are following God Himself. If you claim to be following God, then you must be someone who is walking in divine love because God is love.

**2. You can succeed at the art of following by copying a man of God who is following Christ.**

> *Be ye followers of me, even as I also am of Christ.*
> 1 CORINTHIANS 11:1

Paul instructed believers in the Corinthian church to follow him, but only as long as he followed Jesus. Indeed, there are many ministers who are more followers of millionaires, business executives and politicians than followers of God. You will notice from the books they read and cite that they are following these secular people and desire to be more like them than like Jesus. Today, pastors are reading the biographies of American presidents, millionaires and accomplished entrepreneurs.

**3. You can succeed at following a man of God by following *someone who has followed the person* you really want to follow.**

> *Dear brothers and sisters, pattern your lives after mine, and LEARN FROM THOSE WHO FOLLOW our example.*
> PHILIPPIANS 3:17 (NLT)

Years ago, I wanted to be in the miracle ministry. I knew that I would have to follow someone who was already successful at this. So, I decided to follow Kathryn Khulman because she had the greatest miracle ministry I had ever heard of. As a medical doctor, I was highly impressed with the kind of miracles that she facilitated. But there was one problem. I could not find her on this earth because she had already died. I was at a loss.

How could I follow a dead person? How could I give a dead person an offering? How could I speak to a dead person? Was I going to call up her spirit from the dead?

Suddenly, the Holy Spirit enlightened me. "Follow Benny Hinn if you really want to follow Kathryn Khulman." A bright light illuminated my path and instantly, I knew what I had to do. I began a long journey to follow Benny Hinn and to learn all I could about ministering, healing and miracles. This is the principle that Paul was sharing with the Philippians. "You can follow me by following those who have followed my example."

**4. You can become *a follower of a group* of people who are walking in the grace of the Lord.**

> *And ye became FOLLOWERS OF US, and of the Lord, having received the word in much affliction, with joy of the Holy Ghost.* 1 THESSALONIANS 1:6

Instead of following one person, you can follow a group of people who walk in a particular way. For instance, you could follow the leaders of a particular church or ministry. You could also follow a group of friends who serve God together.

Many years ago, after I was introduced to Kenneth Hagin, I noticed the people he associated with. People like Kenneth Copeland, Jerry Savelle, Fred Price, Charles Capps and John Osteen were found at his conferences and in his magazines. This group of men of faith became attractive to me and I found myself following them. I found myself reading their books and learning from them because they were an identifiable group I could follow.

**5. You can be successful in the art of following by becoming *a follower of a particular church.***

> *For ye, brethren, became FOLLOWERS OF THE CHURCHES of God which in Judaea are in Christ Jesus: for ye also have*

> *suffered like things of your own countrymen, even as they have of the Jews:* 1 THESSALONIANS 2:14

You can follow a church by studying its leaders, its history, its doctrines, its victories, its crises, its errors and so on. To follow a church properly, by all means, study its history. Many churches undergo amazing transformations as the years go by. A church today is often not anything like what it was a hundred years ago.

The Swiss church a hundred years ago was so vibrant that it was sending young men to die on distant mission fields. Through the efforts of the Swiss church, salvation and Christianity came to entire nations like Ghana and Nigeria. Today, the Swiss church is so dead that most congregations are closed down and Christianity is seen as an activity for foreigners and immigrants.

Today, the Swiss organization that sent missionaries to the world has banished the archives of their great missionary work to a cellar in their office building that has been converted into a hotel!

Conversely, I have learned much from the Methodist Church. I have followed many of their good examples and studied the life of their founder. In following that church, God has given me great insight and direction for my ministry.

**6. You must become a follower of *good things* that the Holy Spirit shows you.**

> *And who is he that will harm you, if ye be FOLLOWERS OF THAT WHICH IS GOOD?* 1 PETER 3:13

You must follow good things. If the Holy Spirit touches your heart about something good in another person's ministry, you must consider that God is drawing your attention to something you need to do. The Holy Spirit is always showing us good things that we must follow. It is up to us to open our hearts to notice the good things about other churches and ministries.

Perhaps you notice *how good the music is* in some particular church. Perhaps you *take a liking to the choir.* Maybe you notice *how clean the toilet is* in some church. Perhaps you notice *how good somebody's church structure is*. Perhaps someone's unique style of preaching strikes a tone with you – and, he sings well, to boot! (Wouldn't that be nice?) Maybe it is that that church has a great children's ministry, or you feel you could really get plugged into the singles ministry with minimal discomfort. All these good things you notice may be messages from the Holy Spirit on things you must follow.

**7. You can be successful in following a man of God by following the people they delegate and appoint.**

> *Be imitators of me: FOR THIS REASON I HAVE SENT TO YOU TIMOTHY, who is my beloved and faithful child in the Lord, and he will remind you of my ways which are in Christ, just as I teach everywhere in every church."*
> 1 CORINTHIANS 4:16-17, (NASB)

Paul wanted the Corinthians to follow him closely. For this reason he appointed Timothy and sent him to be with the Corinthians. Anyone who wanted to relate with Paul had to relate with Timothy.

People who cannot relate well with delegated and appointed men do not realise they are losing the opportunity to learn and to follow. People in high demand often have to delegate someone to meet and interact with you. If you decline to interact and relate because you are not dealing with the main person himself, you will lose out on many blessings. The art of following includes the art of following delegated people.

I have been to Korea many times to interact with David Yonggi Cho. I have had to relate with people that he has appointed to care for me and other board members. Happily accepting the people he delegated has been the key to benefitting from my relationship with him. Anyone who deems himself or herself too big to deal with delegated authorities is too big to follow!

**8. You can be successful in following a man of God if you follow his *faith* and his *patience*.**

> *That ye be not slothful, but followers of them who through faith and patience inherit the promises.* HEBREWS 6:12

The two key elements to look out for in a man or woman you are following are faith and patience. Why do I say this? Scripture teaches us that it is the faith and the patience of the person that enabled him to inherit the promises of God.

It is because of Kenneth Hagin's faith and patience that gave him the worldwide ministry that he had. It is Yonggi Cho's faith and patience that gave him the largest church in the world. It is Benny Hinn's faith and patience that gave him his miracle crusades. It is Fred Price's faith and patience that gave him the ministry that he had. It is Reinhard Bonnke's faith and patience that gave him the largest crusades in Africa.

It is not the money, the connections nor the advertisements that gave these people the things that they had. It is their faith and their patience that gave them what they received.

Dear friend, do you want to be successful in the art of following a man of God? Then model his faith and his patience! What does it mean to follow someone's faith? To follow someone's faith is to ask, "What did he believe?" and, "Why did he believe the things he believed?" When I was studying the faith of Billy Graham I noticed that he took a quality decision to believe that every part of the Bible is the Word of God. Because of this faith he quotes scriptures as he preaches to sinners. He believes that if these are the words of God, then when they are quoted to people, these words will have great power to save, to heal and to deliver.

How else can you find out more about the faith of a great person? By watching and listening to the things a person said earlier in his ministry! In the latter part of a person's ministry, you will find the impressive fruits of what he has believed. But in the early part of his ministry, you will see and feel the person exercising his faith for great things in God. In the early part of his ministry there is little to see and there is much faith and much proclamation. It is always interesting to see how men stood up in the wilderness and began to believe great things for their ministries.

Follow the faith and the patience of great men and you will be following the right things. Today, some people want to wear the same clothes, the same shoes and drive the same cars as great men of God. The Bible did not say that they inherited the promises through their cars, their houses and their clothes! They inherited the promises through their faith and their patience!

So then, how can you follow the patience of someone? You can study the patience of someone by finding out when he began to believe certain things and when he actually experienced them. When you start calculating and finding out the number of years that people have believed and worked in a particular direction, you will be amazed at how patient some of them have been.

Most men and women of God have laboured for many years with little results only to see the Lord doing great things toward the end of their lives and ministry. Indeed, the faith *and* the patience of these people is the secret to their ministry.

**9. You must overcome laziness, slothfulness and inertia in order to follow someone successfully.**

> *That ye BE NOT SLOTHFUL, but followers of them who through faith and patience inherit the promises.*
> HEBREWS 6:12

Would you believe that laziness is the reason many cannot follow? I have listened to lazy people who do not want to follow and learn. They say things like:

- "Wow, you have the grace of God upon your life."
- "It is a grace that God has given you to have these churches."
- "I like the way you do things. It is a grace that you have."
- "I don't have the grace that you have. It is not my calling."

Yes, it may be true that the grace of God is at work. But often, people are simply too lazy to learn something new! They cannot be bothered to implement ideas and principles they see working. Indeed, it takes a lot of energy to become like someone ahead of you. It takes a lot of time and earnest effort to discover the secrets of a leader and emulate them. Lazy people cannot and will not be successful in the art of following.

# CHAPTER 3

# Seven Ways to Practice Following

An adage often spoken as encouragement to me as a child declared, "Practice makes perfect." Sometime later I heard the phrase modified to say, "Practice makes permanent." This version is also true, and highlights a vital truth -- it is important to be very careful about the behaviours and skills one decides to practice.

When a believer follows Jesus, knowing what to practice is of paramount importance, and fortunately we're not left to guessing about what to choose. Here are seven markers to guide you in deciding where to place your focus as you practice the art of following after Christ -- seeking to both perfect and make permanent your daily walk with him.

## Follow what Jesus Christ taught and did

*The former treatise have I made, O Theophilus, of ALL THAT JESUS BEGAN BOTH TO DO AND TEACH,* Acts 1:1

The teachings of a person and the things he does are equally important.

To follow Jesus Christ you must follow both his teachings and the things he did. Each Gospel contains the teachings of Christ as well as the stories of the things He did. In some bibles, the teachings of Christ are printed in red and the things He did are in black.

It is important to understand that these two aspects are very different but very important. There are many things Jesus Christ did not teach about. Indeed, there are many things He did without explaining what He was doing. That is why Theophilus was advised to learn from both what Jesus did and taught.

## Follow men of God by following their teachings

It is important that you understand that some people are gifted to teach what they know. This results in them sharing many teachings, doctrines, codes and ideas. For instance Kenneth Hagin, a great prophet and healing minister, taught extensively about how he practiced the ministry and how he achieved great things for God. I have been able to learn much about the ministry by gleaning from his teachings. There were other great prophets who lived and died in the same era, but did not leave any teachings that would guide others into a similar ministry.

## Follow men of God by following what they do

There are people who have done great things for the Lord but have left behind very few teachings about how they accomplished what they did. For instance, Kathryn Khulman had a great miracle ministry that I admire and have learned from. But I have not been able to discover how to enter the miracle ministry through her teachings. However, studying the things Kathryn Khulman actually did has helped me greatly. Reading her biography over and over again has given me many insights into what she actually did in the healing ministry.

Even though I have tried earnestly to learn from the teachings of John Wesley, I have not been able to understand much from his teachings. Indeed, even how he uses the English language is different. However, his life, his challenges and his problems have been such a blessing to me. I have learned so much from what he did, but almost nothing from what he said. You must be able to identify those who are called to teach you by their lives and not by their teachings. Do not be worried if you do not learn from somebody's teachings. Perhaps it is his life that will minister to you.

His life (what he did) consists of his family life, his habits, his marriage, his ministry, his friendships, his associations, his achievements, his problems, his crises, his sorrows and his pains. All the content of the man of God's life will minister to you. This is how you follow someone; by following the things he did.

## Follow a man of God by following *both* his teachings and his life

Some ministers are so gifted that you will learn from both what they do and what they teach. God may send you someone who has a great message in his teachings as well as in his life.

Jesus Christ had the most spectacular teachings ever known to man. Yet His life held even more gems and revelations for mankind. Jesus' cross and experience on the Calvary road spoke louder than any teachings He could ever have given on the subject of obedience and sacrifice.

## Follow people that lived in Bible times

People like David, Abraham and Joshua are given to us to learn from and to follow. They inherited the promises of God and obtained good reports. Their lives are open books for us to learn from. Everyday when you read the Bible you can learn from something Abraham did or what David did.

Because the Bible was not written to impress anyone, it contains the realities of people's lives. Nothing much is covered up and we are ministered to by their lives as they experienced them.

## Follow people who have lived since Bible times

People have served the Lord throughout the many generations since His earthly ministry. These people, whose lives and stories have been written about, are powerful examples that you will be able to relate with.

I have been particularly blessed to follow the life and ministry of several of God's generals who died just a generation before I arrived. People like Kathryn Khulman, William Branham, Jack Coe and A.A. Allen were powerful healing prophets whose lives continually minister to me. I do not see how I could have made it in the ministry without receiving what I have learned from these people. Their names may not be recorded in the Bible but their lives and ministries are very significant to our destiny. Be a believer who reads biographies!

## Follow people who are alive and serving the Lord today

Following people who are currently serving the Lord involves the greatest humility. People love to give the impression that they are self-made and original. They feel particularly demeaned when they have to recognize contemporaries living in the same generation.

People who are alive during your time and generation are often criticised for their lives and ministry. "How could you follow someone with such obvious flaws? You will destroy your ministry by associating with them." But what could be said of my own ministry had I not loved and followed people like Kenneth Hagin, Fred Price, Duncan-Williams, Benny Hinn, Yonngi Cho and Reinhard Bonnke?

Indeed, these living examples have served as a living school, training me for ministry. Their lives, their successes, their trials, their victories and their failures are all great lessons for me. God has used them and continues to use them to disciple me.

It may be you are where you are in ministry because you refuse to learn from people around you.

# CHAPTER 4

# What Jesus Taught About the Art of Following

Have you reflected recently on this?: Whenever Jesus wanted to train someone He said to the person, "Follow me." Notice how He invited Simon Peter, Andrew, Levi, Philip, James, John and many others to follow Him. By his example, Jesus was teaching us that following someone is the highest and best method of training. Look carefully at these six different examples of Jesus asking people to follow Him:

- *And Jesus, walking by the sea of Galilee, saw two brethren, Simon called Peter, and Andrew his brother, casting a net into the sea: for they were fishers. And he saith unto them, "FOLLOW ME, and I will make you fishers of men."* Matthew 4:18-19

- *And as he passed by, he saw Levi the son of Alphaeus sitting at the receipt of custom, and said unto him, "FOLLOW ME." And he arose and followed him.* Mark 2:14

• *The day following, Jesus would go forth into Galilee, and findeth Philip, and saith unto him, "FOLLOW ME."* John 1:43

• *And going on from thence, he saw other two brethren, James the son of Zebedee, and John his brother, in a ship with Zebedee their father, mending their nets; and he called them. And they immediately left the ship and their father, and followed him.*
Matthew 4:21-22

• *And another of his disciples said unto him, "Lord, suffer me first to go and bury my father." But Jesus said unto him, "FOLLOW ME; and let the dead bury their dead."*
Matthew 8:21-22

• *And, behold, one came and said unto him, "Good Master, what good thing shall I do, that I may have eternal life?"*

*And he said unto him, "Why callest thou me good? There is none good but one, that is, God: but if thou wilt enter into life, keep the commandments."*

*He saith unto him, "Which?" Jesus said, "Thou shalt do no murder, Thou shalt not commit adultery, Thou shalt not steal, Thou shalt not bear false witness,*

*Honor thy father and thy mother: and, Thou shalt love thy neighbour as thyself."*

*The young man saith unto him, "All these things have I kept from my youth up: what lack I yet?"*

*Jesus said unto him, "If thou wilt be perfect, go and sell that thou hast, and give to the poor, and thou shalt have treasure in heaven: and COME AND FOLLOW ME."*
Matthew 19:16-21

Jesus also showed us that one must make great sacrifices before he or she can really follow anyone. He told his disciples, "You must take up your cross and deny yourself if you want to follow Me."

> *Then said Jesus unto his disciples, "If any man will come after me, let him deny himself, and take up his cross, and FOLLOW ME."* Matthew 16:24

Jesus showed us that following someone can be a transformative experience. You can be moulded into a completely different person by following. Perhaps God wants to change your destiny. That is why He is showing you someone to follow. Perhaps, God has brought a pastor into your life so that you will have someone to follow. It happened to Simon Peter and Andrew.

> *And Jesus, walking by the sea of Galilee, saw two brethren, Simon called Peter, and Andrew his brother, casting a net into the sea: for they were fishers.*
>
> *And he saith unto them, "Follow me, and I WILL MAKE YOU fishers of men."* Matthew 4:18-19

Following someone can yield many dividends. By following Jesus Christ, the disciples were about to reap houses, lands, brethren, sisters, mothers, persecutions and eternal life. Imagine that! Following Jesus can change your financial situation. Do you think Peter would have inherited lands and houses through his fishing job? Probably not! It is in following Jesus that he received the blessings.

> *Then Peter began to say unto him, "Lo, we have left all, and have FOLLOWED THEE."*
>
> *And Jesus answered and said, "Verily I say unto you, there is no man that hath left house, or brethren, or sisters, or father, or mother, or wife, or children, or lands, for my sake, and the gospel's, but he SHALL RECEIVE AN HUNDREDFOLD now in this time, houses, and brethren, and sisters, and mothers, and children, and lands, with persecutions; and in the world to come eternal life."* Mark 10:28-30

It is very important to recognise what a great privilege it is to be a follower. The choice is not fully yours. While you may want to follow someone, not everyone is invited or allowed to follow.

> *And when he was come into the ship, he that had been possessed with the devil prayed him that he might be with him.*
>
> *Howbeit JESUS SUFFERED HIM NOT, but saith unto him, "GO HOME ..."* MARK 5:18-19

> *And HE SUFFERED NO MAN TO FOLLOW HIM, SAVE PETER, AND JAMES, AND JOHN the brother of James.*
> MARK 5:35-37

Many times have I desired to get close to men of God and have been denied! I have desired to work in the ministry of certain people, but was denied the opportunity. If God has given you the opportunity to follow, and to follow closely, be grateful. Even Jesus did not allow everyone to follow Him.

Another important truth Jesus revealed about following is that many people miss the chance to follow because of their family. If your family is preventing you from obeying the call of God, then welcome to the club. It is not unusual to hear excuses about family obligations. Your family will always be a reason why you cannot and do not obey the call of God. Jesus clearly taught us to put His commandments first. God comes before the family. The family will always pay a price for your obedience. Jesus knows that and He expects you to deny yourself and leave the family and home in obedience to His calling. People who elevate their families above the will of God never fulfil God's calling! Listen to Jesus' sharp responses to people who gave their family obligations as an excuse:

> *And he said unto another, "FOLLOW ME." But he said, "Lord, suffer me first to go and BURY MY FATHER."*
>
> *Jesus said unto him, "Let the dead bury their dead: but go thou and preach the kingdom of God."*
>
> *And another also said, "Lord, I will follow thee; but let me first go BID THEM FAREWELL, WHICH ARE AT HOME at*

> *my house."*
>
> *And Jesus said unto him, "No man, having put his hand to the plough, and looking back, is fit for the kingdom of God."*
> LUKE 9:59-62

So, as one who desires to be Christ's disciple -- to follow and be discipled by Him -- are you prepared to be a good follower? Have you fully counted the cost? These are profoundly important questions. So must be your answers as well!

CHAPTER 5

# The Art of *Not* Following

The Scriptures teach us that as we practice the art of following, there are also things not to follow. This warning is important because evil is usually very popular and so very easy to follow. As believers, we must be single-minded and know what we are determined not to follow.

> *THOU SHALT NOT FOLLOW A MULTITUDE TO DO EVIL; neither shalt thou speak in a cause to decline after many to wrest judgment:* EXODUS 23:2

The first and most obvious warning is not to follow the crowd. The crowd is often wrong. The crowd often does evil.

Remember the children of Israel as they wandered in the desert en route to the land God had promised to give them. At one point, as they approached "the Promised Land" to enter and conqueor, Moses sent ahead twelve spies, including Joshua and Caleb, to scout it out and report on what the challenges might be. Ten of the spies came back with a bad report. They said their enemies were giants and that their kingdoms were too well fortified. The Israelites would not be able to defeat them.

This was the "majority" report and despite the miracle-filled deliverance God had just given Israel from Egypt, the crowd actually wanted to go back into captivity. But the crowd was wrong. Joshua and Caleb delivered the "minority" report and they were right. This is just one of the many places the Bible teaches us not to follow the crowd or the multitudes.

Today, we place a high value on democracy. But for all its benefits, it has an inherent weaknesses for deception and hypocrisy. This is because it is rooted in majority rule -- following the crowd. Democracy depends upon the collective opinion of the multitudes and this can be and often is a very dangerous thing. You must be someone who stands up for what you believe even when the majority does not believe it. If I had followed the majority opinions expressed to me at the time, I would not be in the ministry today.

## Empty people who just talk

> *He that tilleth his land shall be satisfied with bread: but HE THAT FOLLOWETH VAIN PERSONS is void of understanding.* PROVERBS 12:11

Another warning the Bible gives is not to follow vain persons. A vain person is an empty or useless person. Empty people may be businessmen, pastors or politicians, but they all have one main characteristic -- there is nothing of real substance to them! There is a lot of impressive talk, but it is followed by little or no action.

It is amazing that many of the people who have the gift of speaking are actually men of straw. It is a joy to watch them speak. You will follow them to the moon when you listen to their speeches, but in reality they do not even have a car to take you just across town.

Don't be impressed with men who talk too much. You should become wary when you notice you are listening to or dealing with a person who seems too good to be true.

## People who worship idols

> *NEITHER BE YE IDOLATERS, AS WERE SOME OF THEM; as it is written, The people sat down to eat and drink, and rose up to play.* 1 CORINTHIANS 10:6-7

Money is the principal idol of our day and definitely on God's list of cautions. Do not follow people who worship money and do everything for money. Most of this world idolizes money. Of course, money is not inherently evil, but an unhealthy love of it -- idolization of it -- is. Money can be a deceptive trap for the believer.

Watch out for Christians who claim to be in business for God while espousing His Word. They often act as consultants to churches and ministries and to provide services for which they charge fantastic fees. Yet, very often, there is no genuine reverence and fear when they deal with the church and its ministers. These so-called Christian businessmen are serving either the money or their God, and far too often it is money! They will do almost anything to get a little extra money.

Many ministries have gone after money -- doing only the things that are profitable and planting churches only in wealthy cities. The poor are left behind when we allow money to guide our church planting efforts.

It is a most natural thing to join the masses and do what everyone else is doing. I know many people who have left their calling and joined the masses to seek their fortunes. What a mistake and what a tragedy! Do not follow idols even though the whole world has gone after them.

## People who criticise and murmur

> *NEITHER MURMUR YE, AS SOME OF THEM ALSO MURMURED, and were destroyed of the destroyer.*
>
> *Now all these things happened unto them for examples: and they are written for our admonition, upon whom the ends of the world are come.* 1 CORINTHIANS 10:10-11

Be careful not to follow a group of murmuring and complaining individuals. **You will be welded to their disastrous future. You will be destroyed with them.** Many people criticise all the time. Their mouths are filled with chronic discontentment and dissatisfaction with everything.

One can hardly blame them because the world is filled with vanity, emptiness and vexation. ***Murmuring is second nature to the majority of people.*** It takes spirituality and obedience to the Scripture to break out of this practice, to break the habit. Murmuring and complaining is everywhere, but you must not be caught up in it.

Satan is the originator of all discontent. He was given a high position in heaven as a chief worshipper and a principal angel. He walked up and down in the midst of the stones of fire. He was exalted in Eden but was not content to be whom God had created him to be.

Discontentment is satanic in its very nature. No matter what, do not allow it into your life. The very fact that it was Satan who brought discontentment into the world should make you fear it and avoid the practice at all cost.

## Fornication and adultery

> *Neither let us commit fornication, as some of them committed, and fell in one day three and twenty thousand.*
> 1 Corinthians 10:8

Fornication may be the most common sin in the world. (Pride? Blasphemy? Lying?) Maybe: "Fornication is one of the most common sins…" The Word of God consistently tells us not to follow people who live in fornication. This is God's word to you and you must not follow the masses. You must purpose to remain a virgin, even if you are the only virgin left in the world, if you are not married. If you have failed, repent and cry out to God for forgiveness. Walk in his grace. Ask him to restore your heart and mind to the emotional state of a virgin

Today, there are very few virgins in the church and even fewer in the world! The only virgins left are airplanes: Virgin Atlantic, Virgin America, Virgin Australia and Virgin Nigeria!!

## Avoid those who exalt themselves against apostles and spiritual leaders

*I wrote unto the church: But DIOTREPHES, who loved to have the pre-eminence among them, received us not.*

*Wherefore, if I come, I will remember his deeds which he doeth, prating against us with malicious words: and not content therewith, neither doth he himself receive the brethren, and forbiddeth them that would, and casteth them out of the church.*

*BELOVED, FOLLOW NOT THAT WHICH IS EVIL, but that which is good. He that doeth good is of God: but he that doeth evil hath not seen God.* 3 JOHN 1:9-11

Satan was the first person to lift himself up against authority -- against the supreme authority of God Almighty. Everyone who exalts himself against God-appointed authority is following Satan. This is why John advised the church: "Do not follow that which is evil."

Spiritual leaders are often attacked and prevented from doing their work. Diotrephes is the quintessential example of opposition to spiritual authority. Entire churches can gang up against their pastor and fight him. You can hardly find a person in this world who has not criticised one pastor or another. *But, be fairly warned, you must not follow that which is evil!*

# PART II

# Following God's Champions

One of the profound reasons we know the Bible is true and inspired by God is how it describes the men and women God chose to communicate and carry out his purposes in this world. The Scriptures describe the great faith and "heroic" actions of these men and women. But at the same time, nothing about them is held back. Their great weaknesses and very human failures are also on full display. We see them, warts and all, as very ordinary, imperfect people just like you and me.

This helps us understand their encounters with God. They become very real, so interesting, so attractive, believable, uplifting, so motivating, helpful, and inspirational to our own spiritual journey. Each of them interacted with the same unchanging God we know and relate to today. In their lives, they experienced the same yearnings, frailties, temptations and desires of the flesh that you and I have today.

The great lessons each of them can teach us are of eternal value to our own souls. God knew exactly what you and I would need when He inspired the writers to pen each story. As the Psalmist David said, "Your word is a lamp to my feet and a light for my path" (Psalm 119:105). Paul told Timothy: "All Scripture is inspired by God and profitable for teaching, for reproof, for correction, for training in righteousness, so that the man of God may be thoroughly equipped for every good work" (2 Timothy 3:16-17).

I want you to grow as a faithful follower of Jesus Christ. So look with me at eleven of God's champion followers. Their names are familiar: **Abraham . . . Isaac . . . Jacob . . . Joseph . . . Moses . . . Joshua . . . David . . . Solomon . . . Nehemiah . . . Esther . . . and Daniel**. More than half are honored in Hebrews Chapter 11, called God's "Hall of Faith."

What may not be so familiar to you are the unique ways I believe each exhibits the traits and practices, the heart and passions of a person seeking after God and a true believer in Jesus Christ. Each one knew and lived the Art of Following.

Get ready. They have mistakes for you to avoid . . . and victories for you to experience!

# CHAPTER 6

# The Art of Following Abraham

It is time to follow the father of our faith. To do so, we must look closely at his life. What did Abraham do that made him such a great man? The Bible teaches that we should follow after people who have successfully inherited God's promises. "That ye be not slothful, but followers of them who through faith and patience inherit the promises" (Hebrews 6:12).

> *And Abram went up out of Egypt, he, and his wife, and all that he had, and Lot with him, into the south. And Abram was very rich in cattle, in silver, and in gold.* GENESIS 13:1-2

Abraham was a successful person. He was married and had children. He was very rich in cattle, silver and in gold. In our day, he probably would have had investments in banks, properties and stocks. Abraham was a person who knew God. The Lord spoke to him many times and answered his prayers. Abraham fought and won some battles in his lifetime.

Finally, Abraham died at a good old age having seen the mercies of God throughout his life. Even when Jesus told the story of Lazarus and the rich man, he mentioned that Lazarus was taken to Abraham's bosom. That meant that Abraham was still an important person even after his life on earth. Some people are only important in this life. In the next world, they become insignificant to society. They are banished to hell to be punished for their sins.

If Abraham were alive today, people would be asking him for an interview. People would want to ask Father Abraham, "How did you do it? What were the secrets of your success? How did you become so famous and prosperous?" We should also want to ask Father Abraham, "Why did God choose you and speak to you?"

Although we are not living in the days of Father Abraham, we have an accurate account of his life and ministry. By studying the Bible, we can learn some of his secrets and principles. Instead of waiting for some false prophet to ask you for the teeth of a lion and the tail of a tiger as payment for his magic, join me now and let us learn and follow the secrets of Abraham's success.

## Abraham Obeyed God

> *Now the Lord had said unto Abram, Get thee out of thy country, and from thy kindred, and from thy father's house, unto a land that I will shew thee: And I will make of thee a great nation, and I will bless thee, and make thy name great; and thou shalt be a blessing: And I will bless them that bless thee, and curse him that curseth thee: and in thee shall all families of the earth be blessed.* GENESIS 12:1-3

The first time we hear of Abraham, the Lord was giving him an instruction. God told him to leave his country and travel to a strange land. Abraham immediately obeyed the Lord. This first and great key of obedience is something that every believer needs to follow. If you obey God, it will bring blessings to your life.

God told Abraham that He would bless him and that everybody who blessed him would also be blessed. God told him that He would make a great nation out of him. **Notice that all the blessings of Abraham were on the condition that he obeyed God's command.**

There are many people in the world, and God has a blessing for everyone. However, the key that makes the blessing manifest is obedience to God. Abraham made the decision of a lifetime. He decided to leave his family and his country and launch out in obedience to God.

In our lives, we are likely to make two or three momentous decisions. These are decisions that change the entire course of our lives. Remember that greatness is dependent on obedience to the voice of God. Blessings are reserved for those who hear and obey.

"And it shall come to pass, if thou shalt hearken diligently unto the voice of the Lord thy God, to observe and to do all his commandments which I command thee this day, that the Lord thy God will set thee on high above all the nations of the earth: And all these blessings shall come on thee, and overtake thee, if thou shalt hearken unto the voice of the Lord thy God" (Deuteronomy 28:1,2).

## Disobedience Leads to a Curse

There are many people who say, "It is difficult to obey God." But it is more difficult to disobey God. Anyone who disobeys the Lord will experience curses and frustrations in his life. Remember the story of Adam. God put him in a garden and told him that he could eat the fruit of every tree except one. Adam disobeyed God and look at where we are today! Adam was cursed and the entire human race was cursed with him.

All men are now cursed to sweat and struggle in their lives in order to make a living. I know of no human being on the earth that is exempt from this curse. The poor man gives several hours of hard labour and is rewarded with very little. Yet, he has to continue to work hard in order to survive. The rich man works twelve hours a day, seven days a week in order to maintain his riches. He sweats as much as the poor man, but in a different way. All of us struggle under this curse.

Women have been cursed to desire husbands, although their husbands will rule over their lives. I have rarely seen a woman who does not want a husband. "Thy desire shall be to thy husband, and he shall rule over thee"

(Genesis 3:16). Husbands rule and dominate their wives, yet women still want to be married! Women were also cursed in childbirth. A woman will tell you that there is no pain like the pain of childbirth.

Where did all these things come from? They are a result of Adam's disobedience! He disobeyed God and his life became frustrated. But we see a second Adam -- Jesus Christ -- who obeyed God and brought in many blessings. "…so by the obedience of one shall many be made righteous" (Romans 5:19).

Jesus was obedient to His Father. One act of obedience has brought so much healing to the human race. A lost and dying world now has a life in Jesus Christ. God has highly exalted Jesus and given him a name above every name. Exaltation comes through obedience. If you want to be promoted in your life, begin to obey the Lord. Promotion comes through obedience to the Word of God.

As I said earlier, a person will probably make two or three major decisions in his lifetime. (When was this said earlier?) A good example of a major decision is the decision of whom to marry. If you obey God concerning marriage, your life may be relatively peaceful. If you marry the wrong person, unhappiness will follow you like a never-ending stream.

Many people do not obey God when they get to the threshold of marriage. They listen to the flesh and to the opinions of friends. One thing that will influence your state of happiness more than anything else is your marriage. You can never escape the reality of whom you are married to. When you come home, you will meet your marriage partner. When you go out, everything you do will be related to the fact that you are married. If you obey the Lord, He will establish you with His blessing.

## Momentous Decisions of Obedience

A momentous decision to obey God was my decision to be in full-time ministry. On the 10th of March 1989, I qualified as a medical doctor. After seven years of hard labor, I had arrived at a point where many people in the world would have liked to be. I was now a medical doctor! Nevertheless, the Lord told me to leave the medical practice and do His work full-time. I obeyed Him and that decision has changed my life completely.

One day while standing in Jerusalem, I wondered, *How did I get to be in this place?* The Lord told me, "It is because you are following my voice that I brought you here." You do not know the far-reaching effects of obedience to the Lord. Sometimes I stand in church and see all the people whose lives have been changed and I wonder, *Would these people have been saved if I was a practising doctor in a clinic somewhere?* Sometimes we don't have any idea of the effects of our obedience.

I think that many people will not know the effects of their disobedience to God until they get to heaven. I think some people will get to heaven and be told, "There are sixty nine thousand people who were supposed to be in heaven through your ministry! They are all in hell right now, because you refused to obey my call."

They will answer, "Oh, I thought it was just a little teaching in Sunday school that you wanted me to do. I felt that if I didn't do it, someone else would be able to."

That little thing that God wants you to do has a snowballing effect. It will lead to the salvation of many souls. Just do it and be blessed! Obedience is the first key to Abrahamic success.

## Total Obedience

When you do decide to obey God, do not obey him partially. Do not add on things that God did not ask you to do. God did not call Abraham with Lot. He called Abraham alone.

> *Look unto Abraham your father, and unto Sarah that bare you: FOR I CALLED HIM ALONE, and blessed him...*
>
> Isaiah 51:2

Abraham made the mistake of taking Lot with him. This caused Abraham many problems. You see, we do not always understand God's instructions. God was trying to separate Abraham from his family. He was trying to set up a special line and a special person through whom He would bless all the nations of the earth.

The mistake Abraham made is the same mistake many make when they are launching out in ministry. They long to take people with them. They try to form partnerships that God has not ordained. As far as ministry is concerned, God does not call a group of people. He calls a man!

> *And I sought for a man among them...* EZEKIEL 22:30

The Bible doesn't say that God sought for a group of men. God deals with us as individuals. God sought for a man.

## Going with a Partner

Years ago in Ghana, there were not many vibrant charismatic churches. However, there were many vibrant singing and drama ministries. With the passage of time, God began to call some of the members of such groups into the pastoral ministry. Many of the leaders of these ministries were led to establish churches. However, some of these people made the mistake of launching out as a *group* into the church world.

> *So Abram departed, as the Lord had spoken unto him: and Lot went with him...* GENESIS 12:4

That was a big mistake! God was not calling a group. He was calling an individual. Many people who were generally called to be successful pastors had their ministries stifled by the people they took along with them. You see, many of these people who were taken along felt that they had equal power and an equal say with the leader. Executive committees ran the singing and drama ministries, but a committee cannot run a church. A church needs a strong leader supported by wise and loyal assistants.

As you read the Bible, you will notice that there was a time when the servants of Lot quarrelled with the servants of Abraham. Lot did not tell his servants that they were privileged even to be with Abraham. He did not remind his followers that it was Abraham who was called and that he (Lot) was just taken along by grace.

Abraham had to settle the dispute. Abraham took the initiative to separate from Lot. When Abraham asked Lot to choose one section of the land, he took the best part and left Abraham, the real leader, with the leftovers.

**Sometimes when you do things as a *group*, the people around do not know who the real leader is.** They think that it is the group effort that is making things work. It was only after Lot was separated from Abraham that God began to fulfil Abraham's call. When you play for more than fifteen minutes with a child he begins to think that you are his age!

Often, when people are launching out in business they should really do it alone, but they go in for partnerships. I have watched many partnerships break up very painfully. If God wants you to set up a factory, go ahead and do it! Believe God to be able to accomplish it. **Sometimes when you get yourself involved with partners who are like Lot, they forget that you are the one who had the vision.** The time may come when they will even drive you out of the business you created. Just decide to obey God and to obey Him fully.

If God has called you alone, go alone. He will bring people to help you. Don't be afraid! Strength is not in numbers; it is in God. Promotion does not come because you are part of a group. Promotion will come because God has called you. Promotion will come because you are obedient!

## Abraham Had Faith in Messages From the Holy Spirit

> *And he believed in the Lord; and he counted it to him for righteousness.* GENESIS 15:6

The Bible teaches us that Abraham believed in God. That is one of the most notable things about him. He is called the father of all those who believe. Because Abraham had faith in God, God was pleased with him. To say that you are walking in faith is to say that you are following Abraham.

Jesus often told those who were healed, "Your faith has made you whole." It was the use of faith that brought the miracles to these individuals.

Poor health and incurable diseases burden many readers of this book. Many have faced difficult financial struggles. Some have special needs children or children living in serious rebellion. Couples may be experiencing "irreconcilable differences" and other "impossible" challenges. Reasons like these are why we need faith. You must know how to believe even when it seems impossible. What do you have to lose? Faith will bring you many blessings! You must choose to believe that God's power will destroy the power of the enemy.

As you read this book, I can show you several reasons why you may not be alive next week.You will find out that there are many reasons why you could be dead by next week. But why think about that? Why live in fear? Why not exercise faith in the goodness of God? Choose to believe that God will keep you.

When you have faith in God's protective power, you please the Father. Believe that God will give you long life. Believe that your children will turn from rebellion to faith. Believe that God will heal you or give you the courage to endure and even conquer anything that might come your way. Believe that your marriage will be restored. Believe that you will live to see your children and your children's children!

Abraham was ninety years old. He had stopped making love with his wife. He was an old man when God told him that he was going to have a child. The possibility of Abraham having a child was zero, but he believed in God. **God was so happy with Abraham because he believed.** God gets really excited when you have faith in His promises!

> *...without faith it is impossible to please Him.* HEBREWS 11:6

Read through the Bible and see how people looked foolish when they believed God. Do not be afraid of looking odd when you step out in faith. By faith are we saved! I promise and predict that in spite of everything, God will select you and superimpose His purpose on your life. *I see God superimposing His blessings on your life in spite of contrary evidence and contradictory circumstances!* God will do this because of your faith.

The more you exercise faith, the more you will please God. But the more you are blessed, the more people will speak against you. The more you prosper, the more people will hate you. Ignore their hatred, keep on and make sure that you please God with your faith. Faith was one of Abraham's key principles for a successful life.

## Abraham Ruled His Own House

If you are following Abraham you must lead your household successfully. One of the reasons why God chose Abraham and blessed him was because Abraham commanded his entire family to serve Him. When God was about to destroy Sodom and Gomorrah, the Lord thought, *Should I inform Abraham about this? Should I speak to him?* Many people would like God to speak to them. So why did God choose to speak to Abraham? The answer is in the Bible. He commanded his entire family to follow after His ways:

> *For I know him, that he will command his children and his household after him, and they shall keep the way of the Lord, to do justice and judgment...* GENESIS 18:19

Many people do not care what happens to their children spiritually. They are concerned that their children attend prestigious schools and universities. In contrast, they take the spiritual development of their children for granted.

I would not like to bring a child into the world that would end up in hell. If you are following Abraham, you must be concerned that your household serves the Lord. It is more important that your children serve the Lord than that they have a good education.

God said, "I know Abraham. He's going to bring his children to Sunday school. He's going to make them study the Bible." Your children should attend Sunday school and learn about David, Abraham, Joshua and Jacob. They must know all the stories of Jesus Christ. They must learn about Absalom, Lucifer and Judas. It is not just mathematics and science that are important!

You cannot attend church and leave your children at home watching demonic films. God wants you to ensure that your entire household is serving Him. God worked with Abraham because He was confident that Abraham would make his entire family serve the Lord.

If you are a young man, you must marry a Christian. Some people marry women who are not even Christians. Some men just marry a wife because she is fair and beautiful. Yes, she may be that, but she may be spiritually empty. You must marry someone who knows the Word and walks in the Spirit.

God said, "I know Abraham, he's going to marry a believer. He's going to teach them about Me and My ways." God wants you to attend church with your spouse. Some Christian men allow their wives to get out of control. They come to church on their own while their wives stay at home. They say, "She didn't want to come, so I left her."

You've got to keep your household under control -- visitors and even the dogs and cats must serve the Lord. That is the art of following Abraham.

## Abraham Believed In and Practiced Tithing

The art of following Abraham is the art of tithing. Tithing is giving ten percent of all you earn. In every church, there is always a small percentage of people who tithe. You may also have noticed that it is only a small percentage of people who prosper. Tithing is a secret that is hidden from many people. Abraham paid tithes to Melchizedek.

> *And blessed be the most high God, which hath delivered thine enemies into thy hand. And he gave him tithes of all.*
> GENESIS 14:20

Melchizedek was a priest of the most high God. He represented God and the Church. All successful people, who have walked with God, know that it is God who gave them what they have. When King David gave an offering he said, "I'm only giving you what You first gave me."

> *But who am I, and what is my people, that we should be able to offer so willingly after this sort? For all things come of thee, and of thine own have we given thee.* 1 CHRONICLES 29:14

When you realise that it is God who gives you something, you will always want to acknowledge Him. Nebuchadnezzar the king came to a place in his life where he began to boast about what he had. God does not like people who boast about things that were given to them. God does not like it when people boast about what they acquired by grace. God struck him down with a disease that made him think he was an animal. For seven years, he played in the grass like an animal. When he came back to his senses, he gave the glory back to God.

Wherever you are in life, remember that God has made you what you are. Are you intelligent? Are you skilled? Are you beautiful? Everything is from God. "For who maketh thee to differ from another? And what hast thou that thou didst not receive? Now if thou didst receive it, why dost thou glory, as if thou hadst not received it" (1 Corinthians 4:7)?

When God elevates you to a position of influence and authority, please remember that you are there by the grace of God. Every powerful position has an expiration date.

Belshazzar -- another king -- learned this lesson the hard way. He was so happy in his palace that he sent for drinking glasses from the church!

> *Belshazzar the king made a great feast to a thousand of his lords, and drank wine before the thousand.* DANIEL 5:1

He didn't just want to drink wine. He wanted to drink wine from the holy vessels.

He wanted to desecrate the Lord's name. And he did just that.

> *Belshazzar, whiles he tasted the wine, commanded to bring the golden and silver vessels which his father Nebuchadnezzar had taken out of the temple, which was in Jerusalem; that the king... and his concubines, might drink therein.* DANIEL 5:2

That was a mistake! He drank wine from the holy vessels.

> *Then they brought the golden vessels that were taken out of the temple of the house of God, which were at Jerusalem; and the king, and his princes, his wives, and his concubines, drank in them. They drank wine, and praised the gods of gold, and of silver, of brass, of iron, of wood, and of stone.* DANIEL 5:3, 4

Every position you hold in this life is by the grace of God. If you do not decide to give glory to God, He will divinely *displace* and *replace* you. One of the ways a successful person can give glory to God is by acknowledging the grace of God and paying tithes. Do you have Power? Money? A husband? A wife? A house? Cars? A position? You must remember that these things are from the Lord.

Abraham knew that secret. He knew that he had to acknowledge God for his success in life, so he gave tithes. If you want to follow Abraham you must learn how to pay tithes. I want you to notice a great blessing that came unto Abraham after he paid his tithes. God gave him a child. God was stirred to give more blessings to Abraham.

> *AFTER THESE THINGS [PAYING HIS TITHES] the word of the Lord came unto Abram in a vision, saying, "Fear not, Abram: I am thy shield, and thy exceeding great reward…" And behold, the word of the Lord came unto him, saying, "This shall not be thine heir; but HE THAT SHALL COME FORTH OUT OF THINE OWN BOWELS SHALL BE THINE HEIR."* Genesis 15:1, 4

This was the first time that God specifically told Abraham that he was going to have his own special child which would not be his servant's child. Abraham had everything in the world, but he didn't have a child. God knows what you don't have. He knows where your need is greatest. He gave Abraham what he could not buy with money.

Abraham was a great man, he was successful and rich, but he didn't have everything. He didn't have a child. He was so powerful that he had his own private army. His private army had just fought and won a war. How many people on earth today have their own private armies? Abraham had wealth, prestige and long life but he didn't have a child.

Please read your Bible and see for yourself whether what I am saying is true or not. In Genesis 14 Abraham paid his tithes and then in Genesis 15, in the very next few verses, God told him that he was going to have his miracle. **God blesses those who pay tithes.** Go into a church and find out those who have been paying tithes consistently for years. Their lives are different from those who have not been paying tithes. Come to the Lord and honor Him every month.

> *Honor the Lord with thy substance, and with the firstfruits of*

> *all thine increase: So shall thy barns be filled with plenty, and thy presses shall burst out with new wine.* PROVERBS 3:9

God gave you the job you have. Successful people know that and respect that fact! The first fruit is for the Lord. Paying a tithe is not something you should be reminded of. The fact that you are alive ought to be a reminder to you to pay tithes. When you give tithes to God, you become more spiritual. It makes you more committed. When your treasure is in the house of the Lord, you become interested in the church.

> *For where your treasure is, there will your heart be also.*
> MATTHEW 6:21

I think that the reason why some people have difficulties in giving to the Lord is because they do not believe or understand that it is more blessed to give than to receive. If it is more blessed to give than to receive, then those who give have an advantage over those who receive.

If it is more blessed to give, then those at the receiving end are at a disadvantage (relatively speaking). The so-called developing world has been receiving aid from Western powers for years. What has it done for them? Very little! The more people give to the Third World, the more their poverty deepens. Many people grapple with this reality to their own destruction.

Even if you have a little, you can still give something. God calculates your giving in relation to what you have in total. He wants you to give in relation to what you have.

> *And there came a certain poor widow, and she threw in two mites… and [Jesus] saith unto them, "Verily I say unto you, that this poor widow hath cast more in than all they which have cast into the treasury: For all they did cast in of their abundance; but she of her want did cast in all that she had, even all her living."* MARK 12:42-44

I see you rising out of poverty, as you become a giver. I see you tithing. I see you paying your first and best fruits to the Lord. I see you joining that small group of people who are successful in this life.

Listen to me: God doesn't need your money! He doesn't need your little offerings. Whether you pay your tithes or not, the Church will go forward. God is just trying to help you. Abraham knew that God needed nothing from him. The Word of God says that the silver, gold and cattle belong to the Lord.

As you read this book, allow your ministry to enter the realm of divine approval and divine promotion. I see God giving you divine promotion as you pay your tithes.

Divine promotion and elevation are yours for the taking if you follow Abraham. Go forward and never go backward. God is taking you from the minimum to the maximum, and from the negative to the positive. Follow Abraham and enjoy great blessings.

## Abraham Interceded

The art of following Abraham is the art of intercession. The Bible teaches us how Abraham interceded for Sodom and Gomorrah. When Abraham prayed for Sodom and Gomorrah, he was following a divine principle. Most Christians are engrossed with their own problems. Many wives are consumed with the problems of their troubled marriages. They want to be prayed for and anointed over and over again, but the problems never seem to go away.

Abraham had his own problems, but he prayed for Sodom and Gomorrah. At this point, he didn't have a child that was not conceived by a concubine.

The problems went deeper. He had so much wealth and he didn't have anyone to inherit it. There were only servants to inherit his life's work. He had no children. Abraham also had marital problems because of a maid he had slept with. In spite of all this, Abraham found time to intercede for Sodom and Gomorrah. His prayer was so sincere and intensive that God agreed to answer his prayers. This prayer was so significant that it was recorded in the Bible.

> *And Abraham drew near, and said, "Wilt thou also destroy the righteous with the wicked?" And he said, "Oh let not the Lord*

> *be angry, and I will speak yet but this once: Peradventure ten shall be found there." And he said, "I will not destroy it for ten's sake."* GENESIS 18:23, 32

I believe that this is one of the keys to Abrahamic success. Forget about your problems and make God's kingdom and God's problems your concern. You will begin to experience supernatural breakthroughs in your life. You will not even understand why God is blessing you.

When you begin to pray for others, you have graduated into another level of Christianity. I know that many successful Christians rarely pray for themselves. They are always praying for and counselling other people.

Most Christians think: *When everything is okay and God has blessed me, I will start to pray for other people.* But what you don't realise is the divine order that must be followed. They are trying to put the cart before the horse, but the cart cannot go before the horse. Seek first the kingdom of God. After putting the kingdom of God first, you can then tackle your own kingdom.

In the Lord's Prayer, the first topic is "Thy kingdom come and thy will be done." The first prayer is not, "Bless me, give me and help me, Lord!"

I often counsel people who need God's help. "Get involved in the work of God. Bury yourself in God's work! Pray for other people! Let other people's problems become your concern!" You will be surprised at how things will take a dramatic turn.

**When God sees that you want to build *His* house, He will be interested in building *your* house.** Many years ago I heard a great man of God say, "If you build a house for God, God will build a house for you." I have found this to be a true and reliable statement. God wants people who concern themselves with His work. Paul said about Timothy:

> *For I have no man likeminded, who will naturally care for your state. For all seek their own, not the things which are Jesus Christ's.* PHILIPPIANS 2:20, 21

Notice from this Scripture, an age-old problem: Everybody was looking out for his own welfare. Nobody really cared about God's work. Everybody was thinking about *himself* and *his own* problems. If you make God's kingdom your primary concern and intercede for people like Abraham did, you will attract God's supernatural blessings.

In 1985, while in the third year of the medical school, I made a decision for the Lord. I decided not to seek academic laurels anymore. I had just finished the second year and had concluded that it was not worth striving for earthly crowns. I remember telling my "beloved," "From now on, I am not interested in qualifying with a distinction from this school. I don't want any prizes. All I want to do is pass my exams," I added. "From now on, I'm going to build God's kingdom and the church."

It was, from that point forward, that I began to develop into a pastor and eventually established the church Lighthouse Chapel International. It is interesting to note that when I made the decision not to seek great academic laurels, I ended up getting distinctions and winning awards.

You see, in the kingdom, the way up is the way down. In the kingdom, the way to get is to give. In the kingdom, the way to solve your problems is to solve God's problems. Have you ever read about Job? He had more problems than any of us. Job had friends who needed spiritual help. He decided to pray for his friends and look at what happened!:

> *And the Lord turned the captivity of Job, WHEN HE PRAYED FOR HIS FRIENDS: also the Lord gave Job twice as much as he had before.* Job 42:10

Who got the blessing when Job prayed? Who was being prayed for? It was the friends of Job who were being prayed for. But when God moved, it was *Job's* problems that were solved! Is that not amazing? Job got the blessing when he made intercession for his friends. Isn't that interesting?

You pray for *others* and *you* get the blessing! This is an eternal principle. This is one of the principles of success. Husbands, wives, and business-people, please turn your attention to the things of God. In Abraham's day, God's major concern was the deplorable state of the nation Sodom and Gomorrah. Abraham made that *his* problem and prayed earnestly about it. Because of this, God blessed Abraham above all men in his generation.

This is one of the keys to a successful life on this earth. Seek first the kingdom of God! Intercede for others! Help other people! Build God's church! Build a house for God and God will build a house for *you*!

## Abraham Took Up His Cross

God had blessed Abraham with a child. After this, Abraham faced the ultimate test: God asked him to sacrifice his only son. That was a very big request from the Lord. God wanted to see whether Abraham was ready to give up everything for Him.

I believe that God wants to have you as His own. Abraham is not the only believer God will strongly test. I believe that every Christian will have an "Isaac" that God will ask for one day. Will you be prepared to give up your Isaac? You can only give up your "Isaac" if you are fully surrendered to God.

When you begin to walk with God, He will ask you about all the "Isaacs" in your life. He may start with music. Next, He may ask you to give up some friends. Then He may ask you to give more time to Him. Perhaps I should warn you, do not let anything become too precious to you.

Anything that becomes too precious will attract the attention of the Lord and He may ask for it. God wants to be the only God in your life. Our God is a jealous God. He hates the very smell of idols.

*Little children, keep yourselves from idols. Amen.*
1 JOHN 5:21

## A Vision of Gold

Many years ago, when I started out in ministry, the Lord gave me a vision. I was walking on a long and winding path. On this path I saw heaps of some substance which looked like heaps of sand. As I kept walking on the path, I got closer to one of the heaps and discovered that it was a heap of gold. I immediately felt like stopping and gathering as much of it as I could. But I heard the voice of God telling me, "Don't! Stop! Keep on walking!"

Then God told me, "This is the road of ministry for you. As you walk on it, you will meet many such heaps of gold." He said to me, "Don't stop at the gold. The gold is not important." He continued, "There are many such heaps further along. Why should you stop at one of them and settle there?"

Since that time, money has, in a certain way, lost its importance to me. I only see money as a tool. I see it as something I will meet along the way. It is not something I must search for and pile up.

God gave me that vision to help me to see Him as being more important than anything else. I realised that just following the Lord in itself would lead to a supply of all my needs. As soon as something becomes too precious to you, it becomes a potential idol. **The Lord did not want Abraham to replace the love of God with the love of Isaac.**

Dear friend, Abraham was about to become the father of many millions of children. Before God could trust him with such a blessing, He had to make sure that the blessing would never replace his love for God.

**Before God can bless you in a special way, He needs to be sure about you.** Don't hold back anything from the Lord! Give it all to Him and He will make you a great and successful person in this life! Follow Abraham into greatness and receive a permanent blessing in your life.

CHAPTER 7

# The Art of Following Isaac

## Isaac allowed his father to choose a wife for him

*And Abraham said unto the eldest servant of his house, … thou shalt go unto my country, and to my kindred, and take a wife unto my son Isaac.* GENESIS 24:2-4

Let's face it. Most of us did not did not know what we were choosing when we chose our wife. I have been married for more that twenty-two years and I can see the immaturity of the season of my life in which I chose her.

You know more about choosing a wife after you have chosen one and been married for some time. When I see younger people falling in love and being absolutely enchanted by the wrong people, I marvel at the blindness that is so pervasive in a young person. Yet, young people are so sure of their bad choices when they make them, it is almost impossible to speak a word of sense into their heads at that time of their lives.

It takes the highest kind of wisdom to allow someone as knowledgeable as your father to choose a spouse for you. Most of our modern young people would not accept such an idea. I doubt if I would have accepted such an idea when I was getting married. At that stage, I also thought I knew everything and I would not have been open to any suggestions about whom to marry.

The reason why we are able to catch wild animals is because they never vary their activities and never shift from their basic instincts. You rise above the level of an animal when you do things that are not based solely on your instincts.

One day, I responded to a young man's request to help him choose a wife. I told him who I thought would be a good match. As I gave him the advice, I wondered at how differently my mind worked because I was older and more experienced. The art of following Isaac is the art of leaning on the wisdom of the elderly and the experienced.

Most of the unmarried people in the church would have spouses if they would listen to their pastors. But they won't listen, so they live out their lives without experiencing certain blessings.

## Isaac overcame the crisis of not having a child

> *And Isaac was forty years old when he took Rebekah to be his wife, the daughter of Bethuel the Syrian of Padanaram, the sister to Laban the Syrian.*
>
> *And ISAAC INTREATED THE LORD FOR HIS WIFE, because she was barren: and the Lord was intreated of him, and Rebekah his wife conceived.* GENESIS 25:20-21

In spite of your godliness and righteousness you will be required to go through life's crises. This should not surprise or amaze you because we are also called to suffer for Christ. In the Book of Daniel, you see how people of understanding go through trials to make them pure and to purge them of delusions and other evils.

> *And some of THEM OF UNDERSTANDING SHALL FALL, TO TRY THEM, AND TO PURGE, AND TO MAKE*

> *THEM WHITE, even to the time of the end: because it is yet for a time appointed.* DANIEL 11:35

Not everybody is going to have a child. The crisis of not having a child will come to you in one way or another. It may not happen to you personally but it may happen to your son or to your daughter. It may come to your friend, your sister, or a church member that you pass in the halls. In one way or another you will encounter this problem while on earth.

Like Isaac, you have to overcome this problem. Isaac entreated God. This means that Isaac prayed. You must also pray and trust God. Sometimes, the fight to have a child will result in a miracle child. Sometimes, it will not result in having children. God is the giver of children and it rests with Him. We do not understand everything, but our trust and faith must be in God.

You are not the only one who has fallen into this crisis. God has a plan for you. You must follow the example of Isaac and entreat God.

## Isaac Lived In the Will of God

> *And THERE WAS A FAMINE IN THE LAND, beside the first famine that was in the days of Abraham. And Isaac went unto Abimelech king of the Philistines unto Gerar.*
>
> *And THE LORD appeared unto him, and said, "GO NOT DOWN INTO EGYPT; dwell in the land which I shall tell thee of:*
>
> *SOJOURN IN THIS LAND, and I will be with thee, and will bless thee."* GENESIS 26:1-3

Isaac was living where he was because it was the will of God for him. Most people live where they do for financial reasons. To live in a particular place because of the will of God and not because of money is the art of following Isaac.

Like everyone else, Isaac was about to leave the country because of the famine (financial difficulties). This is what most ordinary people do. To move into the higher dimensions of God's will, you must not be guided by money but by the will and decisions of the Lord.

## Isaac Flourished In a Poor Country

> *Sojourn in this (poverty and famine-stricken) land, and I will be with thee, and will bless thee.* Genesis 26:3

Think about it. God instructs you to dwell in a poverty and famine-stricken land. How wise can that be when everyone is migrating to greener pastures? The best place to be is not the richest country in the world. The best place to be is to be in the will of God. I have watched people get poorer as they migrated to the rich countries of the world.

True blessings are found in the will of God. If you are willing and obedient, you will eat the good of the land. Whether the land is rich or poverty-stricken, you will eat the good of the land. Isaac prospered because he followed a lot of instructions. The art of following Isaac is the art of living where God tells you to live.

## Isaac Sowed in Peace

> *And he removed from thence, and digged another well; and for that they strove not: and he called the name of it Rehoboth; and he said, "For now the LORD hath made room for us, and WE SHALL BE FRUITFUL in the land."* Genesis 26:22

If you want to follow the example of Isaac you must follow his great example of becoming fruitful by achieving or acquiring peace.

> *And the fruit of righteousness is sown in peace of them that make peace.* James 3:18

The Scripture is clear that the fruit of righteousness is sown in peace for those that make peace. If you want to do the work of God you must achieve a level of peace. Solomon built many great things because he entered into an era of God-given peace. David on the other hand, could not build anything because he was always fighting.

### The Key To Peace

> *Cast out the scorner, and contention shall go out; yea, strife and reproach shall cease.* PROVERBS 22:10

The key to peace is separation. Separation is the master key to achieving peace with something or someone that you have conflict with. Isaac achieved peace by moving away from the people who strove with him. You can achieve peace by moving away from the people that are in strife with you. If you are in constant conflict with a friend, a brother or a pastor, the key to achieving peace is to move away and separate your life from his life. You will then live apart from each other in peace.

If you are in constant conflict with your associate pastor who does not believe in your calling, you must separate from him by dismissing him or asking him to resign. If you are in constant conflict with your senior pastor, you can achieve peace by separating yourself from his ministry. If you are in constant conflict with your spouse achieve peace by separating your things.

Marital conflicts are brought about by Christians trying to merge their lives and do everything together in the same way. You forget that you were successful individuals living totally separate and happy lives. Conflicts come when one wants to sleep but the other wants to get up; one wants to eat but the other does not; one wants to go out but the other wants to stay. An amount of separation within marriage is necessary. Remember that no two human beings will make the same decision in the same way at the same time!

### Marriage is Not Siamese Twin-ship

I remember watching two ladies who were born and joined together as Siamese twins. They were about eighteen years old but they had one liver. They had lived together and shared their liver for eighteen years. They were forced to go to bathe at the same time, eat at the same time, sleep at the same time, go out at the same time, come in at the same time, watch television at the same time, urinate at the same time, go to the Pharmacy at the same time, talk to the same person at the same time … *always*!!

Indeed, the Siamese twins were truly suffering because of their union and they could not bear it any longer. I watched as they came on television, declaring that they were going to have an operation that had never been done before. They doctors going to attempt to separate them even though they had only one liver. The operation was going to take several hours and the chances of surviving the operation were not very high because it was an experiment. The Siamese twins were interviewed before the operation. They were asked whether they really wanted to take the risk of doing the operation. But both of them were sure that they wanted to have the operation.

They said, "We don't mind dying. Life joined together in this way is unbearable and we prefer to die than to continue living in this joint way." That was a revelation to me. I realised that people needed to be free in marriage to live happily. Even though they may be joined in marriage and love each other, it is unbearable to merge every single aspect of your life

It is this absolute merger that is implied and thought of as being the ideal Christian marriage. But I can tell you that people would have more peaceful co-existence if they agreed to have some amount of separation in their activities, friendships and relationships.

## Isaac Spoke Blessings and Curses With Authority

> *Let people serve thee, and nations bow down to thee: be lord over thy brethren, and let thy mother's sons bow down to thee: cursed be every one that curseth thee, and blessed be he that blesseth thee.* GENESIS 27: 29

You may wonder why a good and decent person may ever have to speak a curse. There are some situations where God's servants must use curses to achieve the will of God. Curses come into play because God's servants are often without any power to protect the work they are called to do.

Through the blessings and curses that you speak, you can wage war on the enemy and accomplish great things for God. On a number of occasions the Holy Spirit has led me to protect the church by speaking a curse on destroyers and rebels who were intent on undoing all that had been achieved for the glory of God.

There are many occasions where a servant of God is helpless. Where he has no power to defend himself nor the work of the ministry. Curses are appropriate defences for the delicate work that God has given him to do.

**Moses Used Curses**

When Moses laid the foundation for the nation of Israel he appropriately placed a series of debilitating curses on those who would undo his efforts by disobeying God. Those curses served to unleash waves of power that served to correct the Israelites and bring them back into line.

Moses released a total of one hundred and twenty-four curses that are found from Deuteronomy 26:14 to Deuteronomy 28 verse 68

- There were twelve curses from Deuteronomy 27:14-26
- There were fifteen curses from Deuteronomy 28:15-20
- There were thirty curses from Deuteronomy 28:21-29
- There were twenty-six curses Deuteronomy 28:30-44
- There were twenty-one curses Deuteronomy 28:48-57
- There were twenty curses Deuteronomy 28:58-68

**Joshua Used Curses**

Joshua had to use a curse to establish his work. He had fought a good fight and possessed the Promised Land for the people of Israel. He placed a curse on anyone who would re-build Jericho, which was the first city he had taken.

> *And Joshua adjured them at that time, saying, "Cursed be the man before the LORD, that riseth up and buildeth this city Jericho: he shall lay the foundation thereof in his firstborn, and in his youngest son shall he set up the gates of it."* JOSHUA 6:26

**Isaac Spoke Blessings**

Isaac was powerless to affect the future of his sons by his presence, by his money or by his decisions. So he used the only power that he had and spoke words of blessings.

> *"Bring me venison, and make me savoury meat, that I may eat, and bless thee before the LORD before my death."*
> GENESIS 27:7

The power of your word is real. You must believe in the power that comes through your declarations and confessions. These declarations and confessions form the blessings or curses that are your weapons.

Notice how the words of the angel strengthened Daniel. Daniel declared, "I have been strengthened because you spoke to me." He revealed how he had been strengthened because of what was spoken to him. People will be strengthened when you speak good words to them. And he said, "O man of high esteem, do not be afraid. Peace be with you; take courage and be courageous!" Now AS SOON AS HE SPOKE TO ME, I RECEIVED STRENGTH. May my lord speak, for you have strengthened me" (Daniel 10:19, NASB).

**Three Times Isaac Spoke a Blessing**

1. "Therefore God give thee of the dew of heaven, and the fatness of the earth, and plenty of corn and wine: Let people serve thee, and nations bow down to thee: be lord over thy brethren, and let thy mother's sons bow down to thee: cursed be every one that curseth thee, and blessed be he that blesseth thee" (Genesis 27:28-29).
2. And Isaac his father answered and said unto him, "Behold, thy dwelling shall be the fatness of the earth, and of the dew of heaven from above; and by thy sword shalt thou live, and shalt serve thy brother; and it shall come to pass when thou shalt have the dominion, that thou shalt break his yoke from off thy neck" (Genesis 27:37-40).
3. And Isaac called Jacob, and blessed him, .... "And God Almighty bless thee, and make thee fruitful, and multiply thee, that thou mayest be a multitude of people; And give thee the blessing of Abraham to thee, and to thy seed with thee; that thou mayest inherit the land

wherein thou art a stranger, which God gave unto Abraham" (Genesis 28:1-4).

## Isaac Overcame the Deception Around Him by Faith in God.

*And Isaac his father said unto him, "Who art thou?" And he said, "I am thy son, thy firstborn Esau." And Isaac trembled very exceedingly and said, "Who? Where is he that hath taken venison and brought it me, and I have eaten of all before thou camest, and have blessed him? Yea, and he shall be blessed."*
GENESIS 27:32-33

Isaac was deceived by his son Jacob. Jacob lied to him and told him that he was Esau. But by the power of God the deceptions that were launched against him could not affect the will of God for his life.

A believer and leader must realise that people around you are always playing one game of deception or another. Some tell outright lies; some play upon your vanity -- praising you somewhat dishonestly; others live hypocritical lives -- presenting to you only one side of themsleves. Most people play upon the vanity of a believer and leader knowing that he or she longs to be seen as a great and successful person.

Through the power of God, none of these deceptions are going to work against you. But the deceptions unleashed against you will turn out for your good and will work out the will of God.

## Isaac Made the Most of His Inheritance

*And Abraham gave all that he had unto Isaac.* GENESIS 25:5

Isaac successfully inherited his father's ministry. He did not destroy the wealth that he inherited from his father. Isaac was not like Rehoboam, who inherited everything from Solomon but lost it within five years.

*And it came to pass in THE FIFTH YEAR OF KING RE-*

> *HOBOAM, that Shishak king of Egypt came up against Jerusalem: and he took away the treasures of the house of the Lord, and the treasures of the king's house; he even took away all: and he took away all the shields of gold which Solomon had made.*
> 1 KINGS 14:25-26

**A Common Mistake**

A common mistake of those who inherit wealth is to inherit it without learning the wisdom that created the wealth. Rehoboam inherited the wealth of his father Solomon but did not learn the wisdom of Solomon. His foolishness was seen at his very first cabinet meeting. He displayed a complete lack of tact and wisdom, the very thing that had created the wealth of Solomon! Indeed, it is said that only two percent of those who inherit a fortune are able to make their inheritance grow.

Isaac, on the other hand, received a great inheritance from his father Abraham and continued the tradition by becoming great in his own right. The principles that had made Abraham rich were the same principles that made Isaac rich. If you do not learn the principles that made someone great, you will not be able to sustain the wealth he gives you.

**What Principles Did Isaac Inherit?**

It is obvious that Isaac inherited the principle of blind obedience to Almighty God. Remember that God made Abraham rich as he blindly obeyed him. Isaac did the same thing. When the Lord told him to stay in a land when there was a famine, he was obedient. Through this obedience, Isaac also became rich in his own right. Isaac's greatness was not because of Abraham's riches. It was because he followed the things that made his father great.

There are countless stories of rich children who, unable to maintain their parents' wealth, start stealing. Making the most of your inheritance is the art of imbibing the principles and wisdom of the person from whom you are inheriting wealth. This is the key to making the most of your inheritance.

## Isaac Accepted Delegated Authorities

*And Abraham said unto his eldest servant of his house that ruled over all that he had, "Put, I pray thee, thy hand under my thigh:*

*And I will make thee swear by the LORD, the God of heaven, and the God of the earth, that thou shalt not take a wife unto my son of the daughters of the Canaanites, among whom I dwell:*

*But thou shalt go unto my country, and to my kindred, and take a wife unto my son Isaac."* GENESIS 24:2-4

This world cannot run without delegated authorities -- somebody who is sent on behalf of another. Most of us would love to deal with the boss himself. Unfortunately, it is not always possible to deal with the highest authority. Anyone who cannot relate properly with a delegated authority is a disaster waiting to happen!

When God sends His prophets, we must accept them. We have to! We have to make do with the prophets even though we would prefer to relate to God Himself. God has sent us His Son. You will have to go through the Son if you want to have anything to do with the Father. Proud people struggle to relate with delegated authorities.

I have had pastors who followed me and were obedient to what I said. However, when it came to dealing with people, I sent them as my representatives. They made the terrible mistake of getting into conflict with them.

- Some failed when they had to relate with my bishops.
- Some failed when they had to relate with my assistant pastors.
- Some even failed when they had to relate with my secretaries.

Someone said, "As for the Bishop, we have no problem with him. He is our spiritual leader and has never done anything wrong to us. It is the 'elder brothers' who are the problem." They said, "If it was just the Bishop we would have no problem at all." But these people are deluded. To fulfil the will of God you will always have to deal with the people He has delegated.

Isaac successfully related with the person his father delegated. Isaac accepted his father's servant Eliezer of Damascus. Eliezer went to select a wife for Isaac and Isaac accepted it. Some people might accept it if their father chose a wife for them. But how many would accept if a delegated representative chose a wife for them? Most people would feel that the representative would not be capable of choosing the right wife for them.

Through Isaac's humility and the acceptance of the delegated authority, he continued to walk in the footsteps of his father Abraham and continued the line of greatness, becoming one of the patriarchs of both Israel and Christianity.

Many people do not receive the anointing because they will not accept the people God sends to them. Rejecting delegated authority is perhaps the most common mistake of proud people!

CHAPTER 8

# The Art of Following Jacob

## Jacob Did Not Despise His Birthright (Natural Heritage)

*And Jacob said, "Sell me this day thy birthright."*

*And Esau said, "Behold, I am at the point to die: and WHAT PROFIT SHALL THIS BIRTHRIGHT DO TO ME?"*

*And Jacob said, "Swear to me this day," and he sware unto him: and he sold his birthright unto Jacob.* GENESIS 25:31-33

Your birthright is what comes to you because of whom you were born to in terms of your family, your tribe and your country. Your birthright is the right you have because of your birth. By this, I mean something that God has given to you. It may be your skin colour, it may be your tribe and it may be the country you come from. Your natural heritage is what you are born into or what you have because of who your parents are.

Everybody has a birthright. Esau's birthrights were the rights he had because he was the first born of Isaac. Being the first born of Isaac had a lot of implications. He would inherit double the portion of everything that his father owned and become twice as wealthy as everyone else. Esau would dominate his family because of his birthright.

But Esau said, "What profit shall this birthright do to me?" By saying this, he despised his birthright. It is easy to despise your birthright and see yourself as being inferior to some other person who seems to be more blessed than you. If you look carefully, you will discover that there are things loaded into your life because of your birthright. It is time to see what God has given you and stop moaning and wishing that you were like somebody else.

Some years ago, I ventured out into evangelistic ministry. I was really frightened because I knew I would need a lot of money that I didn't have. I listened to Benny Hinn as he described how he used millions of dollars for his crusades. I read about how Reinhard Bonnke equally used millions to hold such large campaigns. I thought to myself, *Where on earth am I going to get such money? I come from Ghana and I don't know any Americans who would give me such amounts of money to hold crusades.*

Then the Lord showed me that He had given me other things because of who I was and where I came from. Because I had grown up in Africa, I knew my way around the African scene much better than any non-African person would ever be able to. I had access to grassroots information and people who would do things for me at a small fraction of what foreign evangelists would pay for. Indeed, my birthright (growing up and living in Ghana was paying heavy dividends for me). I suddenly realised that I was capable of doing many things because of where I had lived.

Esau despised his birthright. Being the first born meant nothing to him. What God had given to him through nature and by birth was of no value to him. He despised it and lost it. Perhaps you are an African who has always wanted to be an American, or vice versa. Maybe you have despised the language, the tribe and the country that God has given you. You have even despised your colour; wishing you were fairer, whiter or blacker than you are. What you do not realise is that all these things are gifts called your birthright.

I used to wonder why I was half black and half white. My brown colour did not seem to fit into Africa or Europe. When I went to America, they called me a black man. When I was in Ghana, I was called a white man. In

Kenya they called me "Point 5." Americans would say to me, "You are an African, aren't you?" And Ghanaian children would shout "obroni" at me as I passed by. "Obroni" means the white man. However, as time passed, I began to see great benefits in my birthright and how God had made me. I have discovered vast regions of the world where I fit in perfectly and where they think I am one of them. What an advantage God has given me in many harvest fields!

## Jacob Pleased His Parents

> *And Isaac called Jacob, and blessed him, and charged him, and said unto him, "Thou shalt not take a wife of the daughters of Canaan...."*
>
> *When Esau saw that Isaac had blessed Jacob, and sent him away to Padanaram, to take him a wife from thence; and that as he blessed him he gave him a charge, saying, "Thou shalt not take a wife of the daughters of Canaan."*
>
> *And that JACOB OBEYED HIS FATHER AND HIS MOTHER, AND WAS GONE TO PADANARAM;*
>
> *And Esau, seeing that the daughters of Canaan pleased not Isaac his father;*
>
> *Then went Esau unto Ishmael, and took unto the wives which he had Mahalath the daughter of Ishmael, Abraham's son, the sister of Nebajoth, to be his wife.* GENESIS 28:1, 6-9

One or several degrees from a university, a great job at the bank or even a very healthy lifestyle cannot undo the curse that comes to children who do not please their parents. Honoring your father is the great and first commandment that comes with a blessing. What many do not realise is that honoring your father involves *obeying* him and *pleasing* him.

A person's obedience to his parents will determine his future. Some people grow up wanting everything about them to be different from what their parents want. Esau was the opposite of Jacob! When he found out what pleased his parents he did exactly the opposite.

Jacob on the other hand, did what he thought would please his parents. Marrying a girl because it pleased his parents was not too much to ask of Jacob; he was that kind of person. Think about that: living with a woman and having children with her because it pleases your parents. That is a big decision to take just because you want to please your parents.

Many people do not do well in life because they do not please their parents. Remember that, when you were born, your parents were pleased to show you off to the world. They were pleased with your coming into the world and they will always want to be pleased with you. Honoring and pleasing parents of all kinds will always be the great divider between those who do well and those who do not do well.

## Jacob Was Wary of A Curse

> *And Jacob said to Rebekah his mother, "Behold, Esau my brother is a hairy man, and I am a smooth man:*
>
> *My father peradventure will feel me, and I shall seem to him as a deceiver; and I SHALL BRING A CURSE UPON ME, AND NOT A BLESSING."*
>
> *And his mother said unto him, "Upon me be thy curse, my son: only obey my voice, and go fetch me them."*
>
> *And he went, and fetched, and brought them to his mother: and his mother made savoury meat, such as his father loved.*
>
> Genesis 27:11-14

Jacob was deeply spiritual; always conscious of the impact a blessing or a curse would make on his life. He valued his birthright, he feared curses and he believed in the power of a blessing. This contrasted sharply with Esau who had no time for such impractical concepts. When his mother asked him to lie to his father, he knew that his father could curse him for telling a lie. His mother, sensing her son's spirituality and reluctance to receive a curse, offered to receive the curse for him. What a shock! Indeed, this was the last time we hear of Rebecca. She had cursed herself out of the history books!

I can find no economic, financial, political or historical explanation to many things in this world, except I explain that it is a result of curses or blessings. I am a firm believer in the power of curses and blessings.

Dear friend, do not take lightly the reality of the power of a curse. The Scripture says, "A curse causeless shall not come." This means that a curse shall not come unless there is a good reason for it. To follow Jacob is to believe in the power of curses and blessings.

## Jacob Knew How to Engage in Prayer Warfare

> *And Jacob was left alone; and there wrestled a man with him until the breaking of the day...*
>
> *And he said, "Thy name shall be called no more Jacob, but Israel: for as a prince hast thou power with God and with men, and hast prevailed."*
>
> *And Jacob asked him, and said, "Tell me, I pray thee, thy name." And he said, "Wherefore is it that thou dost ask after my name?" And he blessed him there.* GENESIS 32:24, 28-29

It is easy to attribute a person's success to his good character, her financial prudence or his oratory skills. However, you will rarely find a true man or woman of God who does not travail in prayer to achieve victories in the Spirit.

This is what Jacob did. He travailed in the spirit world and was successful, spiritually. This spiritual success was what guaranteed him success in his dealings with men.

I once met a brother who looked mystified when I told him that I could pray for seven continuous hours. He was puzzled when I said that I could pray for days on end. He told me that he had never prayed for more than twenty minutes at a go. It is amazing how many believers do not rise up in true spirituality and true prayer.

## Jacob Had A Personal Encounter With God

*And he dreamed, and behold a ladder set up on the earth, and the top of it reached to heaven: and behold the angels of God ascending and descending on it.*

*And, behold, the Lord stood above it, and said, "I am the Lord God of Abraham thy father, and the God of Isaac: the land whereon thou liest, to thee will I give it, and to thy seed..."*

*And Jacob awaked out of his sleep, and he said, "Surely, THE LORD IS IN THIS PLACE, AND I KNEW IT NOT."*

Genesis 28:10-16

Jacob came to a place and had an encounter with God because God was there. Anyone who amounts to something in his or her spiritual life or ministry has had a personal encounter with God. It is this personal encounter that defines him or her. You cannot do well by living on other people's experiences. You can be encouraged by other people's experiences and you can learn from them, but you must have your own personal experience with God. It is only people with a first-hand experience who truly minister the power of God.

Without ever talking to someone you cannot really have authority to talk about him because you do not know him! People who talk about me with authority but have never met me or interacted with me, speak from their own minds and imaginations of what I might be like. Those who say I am humble but have never met me do not really know whether I am proud or humble.

Power and authority come from closeness and from having spoken to someone personally. Jacob had power with men because he had had power with God. He had been close to God and he had spoken to God. From henceforth, his words and actions were going to carry much power.

## Jacob Covenanted To Pay Tithes

*And Jacob vowed a vow, saying, "If God will be with me, and*

> *will keep me in this way that I go, and will give me bread to eat, and raiment to put on,*
>
> *So that I come again to my father's house in peace; then shall the Lord be my God:*
>
> *And this stone, which I have set for a pillar, shall be God's house: and of all that thou shalt give me I WILL SURELY GIVE THE TENTH UNTO THEE."* Genesis 28:18-22

One of the things to follow about Jacob is to follow him in making a covenant to pay tithes. Jacob made a covenant with God, and in this covenant he promised to do three things: he promised to serve God, to build His house and to pay tithes.

There were three main ingredients in the covenant of tithing. It was a covenant that displayed his great understanding of what God does for us. He knew there were three things only God could do for him. Only God could provide his needs, only God could protect him and only God could help him by being with him. In exchange for these, he promised to fully pay his tithes. He was a businessman and knew the implications of a contract.

Most people do not know what God does for them. That is why they fail to tithe everything they have. Many people do not know the invisible power that is released on their behalf as they pay their tithes. He protects us, He provides for us and He is with us to help us in all affairs of life. This is the blessing of the tithe and Jacob understood how great blessing was released through the covenant of tithing.

Tithes are what you owe to the Lord. The tithe is what will cause you to be rich and prosperous. The nation of Israel is rich and prosperous because Jacob (Israel) initiated the tithe and the nation of Israel has continued to pay its tithes. Indeed, God has provided for them, God has been with them and God has helped them.

## Jacob Gave Many Years of His Life to Fulfil His Vision

> *And Jacob served seven years for Rachel; and they seemed unto*

*him but a few days, for the love he had to her.* GENESIS 29:20

*Fulfil her week, and we will give thee this also for the service which THOU SHALT SERVE WITH ME YET SEVEN OTHER YEARS.*

*And Jacob did so, and fulfilled her week: and he gave him Rachel his daughter to be his wife also.* GENESIS 29:27-28

Unfortunately, many people desire to accomplish great things in a few years. They wish to bear fruit and to do that entirely, in just two or three years. But that is not realistic. Real ministry involves your life. It involves your *whole* life. The call of God is such that it needs "a whole life" to accomplish it.

When Jesus died on the cross He gave up His *whole* life. He gave up His youthfulness, his middle age and His old age. If life begins at forty, Jesus Christ was never forty years old to even begin this life. This is why He died on the cross as a young man.

When the Lord tells you to take up your cross and follow Him, He is asking you to lay down your *whole* life. Don't forget this: your ministry will need a *whole* life in order to be accomplished!

Jacob gave up fourteen years of his life to fulfil his vision of marrying Rachel. God had put it in his heart to love Rachel and to desire her. Indeed, it took him many years to fulfil this vision. You will need a lot of time to fulfil the call of God. If you want to be as successful as Jacob, plan to give several of the best years of your life to fulfil God's call and vision. Indeed, no one can achieve much in a few months or years. Ministry takes a "whole life" to be truly realized.

## Jacob Allowed God to Work Things Out Rather Than Doing It Himself

*And he said, "What shall I give thee?" And Jacob said, "Thou shalt not give me any thing: if thou wilt do this thing for me, I will again feed and keep thy flock:*

> *I will pass through all thy flock to day, removing from thence all the speckled and spotted cattle, and all the brown cattle among the sheep, and the spotted and speckled among the goats: and of such shall be my hire.*
>
> *So shall my righteousness answer for me in time to come, when it shall come for my hire before thy face: every one that is not speckled and spotted among the goats, and brown among the sheep, that shall be counted stolen with me."*
>
> *And Laban said, "Behold, I would it might be according to thy word."* GENESIS 30:31-34

This famous story shows Jacob subjecting himself to God's ability to prosper him. He did not ask Laban for five hundred or six hundred sheep as his reward. He subjected himself to the uncontrollable factors of reproduction. He said, just give me any spotted and speckled sheep and goats that are born. What a gamble! If the sheep that were to be born were not spotted and speckled, Jacob would have nothing. Indeed, a much safer contract would have been to ask Laban for five or ten percent of the flock.

Laban, of course, was happy to strike such a deal. He had no idea that God would make the spotted and speckled sheep multiply until most of the flocks were spotted and speckled.

In subjecting himself to these uncontrollable factors of destiny, Jacob subjected himself to God's providing hand. Most of us are not trusting enough to allow God to take control and prosper us the way He wants to. We have to make a move! We have to intervene! We have to interfere with nature! We have to speed things up! But Jacob trusted the Lord for everything. He knew that God would provide for him. To successfully follow Jacob, you will have to trust that God will provide for you.

When people get into difficulty, they claim God did not help them. When their marriages run into difficulty, they say they missed the will of God. It is important to get to the place where you accept the good, the bad and the ugly as God's provision for your life.

When Jacob said, "I will take the spotted and speckled sheep," he was making a statement of the highest kind of trust. He was saying, "However the spotted and speckled sheep turn out, I will accept it as God's will and provision for me. If it is good, I will take it as God's provision for me; if it is bad, I will take it as God's provision for me." Can you leave your destiny in God's hands and accept whatever he gives you?

## Jacob Knew When the Season Had Changed

> *And he heard the words of Laban's sons, saying, "Jacob hath taken away all that was our father's; and of that which was our father's hath he gotten all this glory."*
>
> *And JACOB BEHELD THE COUNTENANCE OF LABAN, AND, BEHOLD, IT WAS NOT TOWARD HIM AS BEFORE. And the Lord said unto Jacob, "Return unto the land of thy fathers, and to thy kindred; and I will be with thee."*
>
> GENESIS 31:1-3

Seasons change all the time, but people do not often recognise when they change. Jacob had lived with Laban for years, but the season had changed. He knew the time had come to move on!

There are many "changes" that do not signal the change of a season per se. Changes in circumstances or attitudes of people do not signify a change in season. To detect a change in season is to have supernatural knowledge from God about when and how you must move on or move ahead.

### The Spirit of Knowledge

When you receive the Spirit of Knowledge you will know a lot of things supernaturally and even instinctively. This is the kind of knowledge that comes from God.

A study of wildlife and nature reveals how God has put knowledge in different animals. Many animals know exactly when to begin their migrations and they know where to go. They accomplish mysterious feats of navigation, endurance and courage as they go through their great journeys across the earth.

Animals are born into the wild and instinctively know how to hunt. Animals know how to copulate without ever being taught what to do and how to do it. These animals never watch pornography or have marriage counselling and yet they know where their sexual organs are and what to do with them. They know when to have sex and how frequently to do it.

For instance, lions know that they must mate up to twenty to forty times a day for several days if they are to achieve a pregnancy. Lions know that they must even forgo eating during that period in order to mate successfully.

Animals know that they must gather extra food and store it up for the winter. They know a season of dryness and hunger is coming and they prepare for it. Creatures as small as ants have knowledge that baffles humans. This wonderful knowledge is God-given and did not come to the animals by learning or reasoning. This is what I call the knowledge of God – the knowledge that comes without learning, reasoning or studying.

Through the Holy Spirit, you will have the knowledge of God, which is the knowledge that comes without learning, reasoning or studying. Through the Holy Spirit, I know certain things without learning them. Through the Holy Spirit, you will know certain things that you did not know by learning or reasoning. Through the Holy Spirit, you will know certain things that you did not know by studying. This is what is called the knowledge of God and it will help you detect a change in the season.

If you are sensitive to the Holy Spirit, you will know all about seasons and how to respond to them when they change. If you do not change when the season changes, you will be found wearing your summer clothes in winter. To follow Jacob successfully you must detect the change in the season of your life and move on.

## Jacob Shaped the Future Through Spoken Blessings

*And Jacob called unto his sons, and said, "Gather yourselves together, that I may tell you that which shall befall you in the last days.*

*Gather yourselves together, and hear, ye sons of Jacob; and hearken unto Israel your father."* GENESIS 49:1-2

Jacob is famous for the blessings and declarations he spoke over his many children before he died. He had come to believe in the power of declared blessings. He knew that God would honor the words of a father when they were spoken with faith. Words of blessing override the effects of your background, your education and your job! Declarations of blessings lift you above the contours and circumstances of this world. When you are about to fail, you will somehow be lifted up by the blessings on your life.

This is the blessing that was proclaimed on Israel. Millions of people have hated them and fought against them. Each time, when it seemed that they would never recover, they miraculously escaped annihilation and became even stronger. The world marvels today as wealthy Jews dominate the financial world.

If you know the power of blessings, you will be cautious and careful in your declarations knowing that they can, and will, happen. I used to pray for and bless pastors and others who left our church. However, I have learned to withhold my prayers until they prove that they are not a dangerous or destructive departee. If you bless a devil, it will prosper and fight against you with the strength that you blessed it with. Spiritual people do not hastily declare blessings on everything and everyone. There are people who have blessed others saying, "*May you triumph over your enemies*," only for these people to become *their* enemies and have the power to triumph over them!

Jacob understood the power of proclaiming blessings and used them effectively to have a successful life.

CHAPTER 9

# The Art of Following Joseph

## Joseph Was Not Provoked By Rejection

*And Joseph dreamed a dream, and he told it his brethren: and THEY HATED HIM yet the more.* GENESIS 37:5

*And he dreamed yet another dream, and told it his brethren, and said, "Behold, I have dreamed a dream more; and, behold, the sun and the moon and the eleven stars made obeisance to me."* GENESIS 37:9

Survival in the Christian life, especially in the long term, is always related to your ability to ride the waves of depraved human character. There are seven unseen rivers that govern almost everything that happens on this earth. These are the rivers of human nature that determine the outcome of many things. Instead of common sense determining the outcome of things, it is these rivers that determine the outcome of almost anything that happens on earth.

For instance, oil may be discovered in a country. The existence of this oil should make everyone in that nation prosperous. But when the powerful rivers of greed and selfishness appear, only a few people get rich and the masses are left in abject poverty.

**Seven human rivers of power**

What are these seven human rivers that govern everything? They are the rivers of greed, selfishness, jealousy, lust, racism, wickedness and the abuse of power. You must not be provoked, misdirected or misled by any of these human rivers.

You must not be easily provoked because that is how to walk in love. "LOVE is patient, love is kind, and is not jealous; love does not brag and is not arrogant, does not act unbecomingly; it does not seek its own, IS NOT PROVOKED, does not take into account a wrong suffered" (1 Corinthians 13:4-5; NASB).

You must not be easily provoked because provocation is a trap that has been set for you. "As Jesus was leaving, the teachers of religious law and the Pharisees became hostile and tried to provoke him with many questions. THEY WANTED TO TRAP HIM into saying something they could use against him" (Luke 11:53-54, NLTSB).

The art of following Joseph is the art of not being easily provoked by the rivers that flow from human nature. The rivers of forgetfulness, wickedness and ungratefulness can turn a cheerful and pleasant person into a bitter personality. It is important that you are not provoked by the ungrateful and selfish human psyche. The wickedness of Joseph's brothers and inability to remember that he was flesh of their flesh and bone of their bone constituted a huge and important river of human nature which Joseph encountered. This river swept him off his feet and carried him to another world where he suffered terribly.

Many things we experience in our lives can and do twist us into corrupted human beings ready to spew out venom that corresponds to the evil we have received. If we received hatred, we are ready with our own version of wickedness. If we received no love, we are ready to live our life showing little care for others. If we received the brunt of the ways of selfish leaders, we are ready to grow up and become worse leaders.

The study of Joseph is a study of how to overcome the diverse provocations that we encounter on earth. The art of following Joseph is the art of overcoming provocation.

You must overcome provocation by continuing to dream in spite of the rivers of rejection. Rejection is one of the rivers you must cross. Few people will go through life without being rejected. You may be rejected in your class, rejected by your friends or, God forbid, rejected by your family. Definitely, people of a different tribe, color or nation will reject you. These are different types of rejection you can experience.

Remember that there are people that will want you or celebrate you, even though you are rejected by others. If you drown when you get to the river of rejection, you have not done well. Many others have been rejected but are still pressing on.

Remember that you can never be fully accepted unless you have first been rejected.

- Don't move away.
- Don't pity yourself!
- Don't think, "No one loves me!"

Even though you have been rejected, someone does love you and there is a place where you will find full acceptance. Maybe you were rejected because of certain deficiencies. Work on those deficiencies. Pitying yourself will get you nowhere. Whenever I am rejected, I say to myself, "Even though I am rejected here, I am loved somewhere else." Like Joseph, I want to persist in having dreams and visions. I repeat: do not drown in the river of rejection.

People I admired have rejected me continuously. What a painful experience it is to be rejected by the person you love, cherish and almost idolize!

I remember a man of God who rejected me in spite of my ardent commitment to him. He treated me like a rebel, even though I loved him and wanted to be close to him. Then he seemed to welcome those whom I knew were disloyal to him. I thought to myself, *What is the use of all my loyalty to this brother?* But I persisted in my visions and dreams.

One day, I mused over the acceptance I seemed to have achieved of this man of God. Then I thought to myself, *It has taken more than twenty years to be accepted of the beloved.*

Be like Joseph. Do not retreat because you are rejected. Rejection is simply one of the rivers you must cross in your journey.

## Joseph Was Not Provoked by Envy and Hatred

*And he dreamed yet another dream, and told it his brethren, and said, "Behold, I have dreamed a dream more; and, behold, the sun and the moon and the eleven stars made obeisance to me."*

*And he told it to his father, and to his brethren: and his father rebuked him, and said unto him, "What is this dream that thou hast dreamed? Shall I and thy mother and thy brethren indeed come to bow down ourselves to thee to the earth?"*

*And HIS BRETHREN ENVIED HIM; but his father observed the saying.* GENESIS 37:9-11

Somebody will hate you. The important thing is not to respond to hatred by becoming hateful yourself. Most hateful people have been hated by someone before. I used to think that people's hatred was a sign of poor Christian character. But I found out that only hypocrites and pretenders are liked by everyone. A really good person must be liked by some and hated by others. If everybody likes you, there is something wrong with you.

Did everyone like Jesus? Certainly not! Was He the Son of God? Yes, He was! But He had lots of people who hated Him. Do not allow the envy and the hatred of people to stop you from serving God. Follow Joseph and persist in your ministry in spite of envy and hatred.

## Joseph Was Not Provoked By Strange Women

*And it came to pass after these things, that his master's wife cast her eyes upon Joseph; and she said, "Lie with me."*

> *But he refused, and said unto his master's wife, "Behold, my master wotteth not what is with me in the house, and he hath committed all that he hath to my hand;*
>
> *There is none greater in this house than I; neither hath he kept back any thing from me but thee, because thou art his wife: how then can I do this great wickedness, and sin against God?"*
> GENESIS 39:7-9

You cannot live in this world without encountering the rivers of immorality, lust, fornication and adultery. You are bound to meet up with them somewhere. You are bound to meet up with pornography, lust, licentiousness, prostitution, fornication, adultery and homosexuality. What are you going to do about this? You must overcome the provocation by continuing to walk in holiness and righteousness. Staying clear of immorality is possible through the grace of God and the wisdom that He will give.

Unfortunately, our bodies are often lusting after things that are forbidden. The great struggle to stay pure must be fought. We must overcome this scourge and emerge victoriously like Joseph did. Joseph persisted in his determination to stay pure from the beautiful temptress we call Potiphar's wife. The art of following Joseph is the art of overcoming the lusts and immorality that are so natural to this human race. You can never say that you are following Joseph unless you overcome immorality in your life.

## Joseph Was Not Provoked By Lies and False Accusations

> *And she laid up his garment by her, until his lord came home.*
>
> *And she spake unto him according to these words, saying, "THE HEBREW SERVANT, WHICH THOU HAST BROUGHT UNTO US, CAME IN UNTO ME TO MOCK ME.*
>
> *And it came to pass, as I lifted up my voice and cried, that he left his garment with me, and fled out."* GENESIS 39:13-18

The devil is the accuser of the brethren and you can be assured that he will accuse you sooner or later. Accusations weaken you and can destroy you. Joseph was falsely accused but he survived this provocation. Most good people are accused of terrible crimes. Sometimes they are accused of the exact opposite of what they are. You must get used to being accused and carry on as though you do not hear all the things that are being said about you.

## Joseph Was Not Provoked By Injustice

> *And Joseph's master took him, and put him into the prison, a place where the king's prisoners were bound: and he was there in the prison.* GENESIS 39:20

Joseph was sent into a prison. He experienced something he did not deserve. Being unjustly treated evokes such strong feelings in almost everyone. You want to rise up and correct the injustice. You want to rise up and prove to everyone that you cannot be easily cheated. But God's way is often that you allow the injustice. "…Why not rather be wronged? Why not rather be defrauded?" (1 Corinthians 6:7, NASB). As you mature, you will realise your need to accept injustices as part of your walk with God. Follow Joseph and accept the injustices of your life and ministry.

## Joseph Used His Gift in Spite of the Difficulties of Life

> *And the chief butler told his dream to Joseph, and said to him, "In my dream, behold, a vine was before me;*
>
> *And in the vine were three branches: and it was as though it budded, and her blossoms shot forth; and the clusters thereof brought forth ripe grapes:*
>
> *And Pharaoh's cup was in my hand: and I took the grapes, and pressed them into Pharaoh's cup, and I gave the cup into Pharaoh's hand."*
>
> *And Joseph said unto him, "This is the interpretation of it: The three branches are three days…"* GENESIS 40:9-15

While he was in prison, Joseph kept himself busy by interpreting dreams. Even prison could not keep him from exercising the gift God had given him. This is one sure way of overcoming the provocation of ungratefulness.

Perhaps there are those who do not remember the things you have done for them. Perhaps they have forgotten so quickly all the labor you have bestowed on them. But this should not be the end of your personal ministry. As you continue to reach out and touch other lives, someone will show much gratitude and this gratitude will far outweigh the ingratitude you have been receiving.

## Joseph Become a Favorite

> *Now ISRAEL LOVED JOSEPH MORE than all his children, because he was the son of his old age: and he made him a coat of many colours.* GENESIS 37:3

It may seem silly or even trivial to want to be your boss' favorite, but it is wise to want to be the most important person's favorite. The most important person is the one who really matters. You will please someone with what you do so why not choose to please the most important person? Who is it that will pay you? Who is it that will feed you? Who is it whose decisions will change your life? Who will promote you? Why not decide to impress that important person!

The world does not only function according to principles but also according to "favor." Favor is when good things are done to you for no apparent reason. Favor is when honor and blessings are bestowed on you even though you do not deserve them.

Somehow, you must develop the art of becoming a favorite while being genuine and unpretentious. I am not talking about being obsequious! I am not talking about becoming a sycophant! I am not talking about getting ahead through flattery, deception or bootlicking.

Even in the army, you can only rise up to a certain level through promotional exams. The really high ranks are attained by what they call "political appointments." These so-called "political appointments" are based on people liking and choosing you. In a government, the president chooses whom he wishes and whom he likes to certain positions. There is often no formula to his choices. The "favorites" are often given key jobs in key positions.

Becoming a favorite of someone is no mean task. It involves understanding what the person likes and doing things that please him. It may sound simple, but different things please people differently. Why not please the one who pays you? Why not impress the person who really matters? Why not do what he likes or wants?

Some bosses are pleased when you start a project well. Others are only pleased when it is finished. Everyone pleases someone! It is up to you to choose *whom* you want to please. Discover what type of boss you have and do everything to make *him* or *her* happy. It is all about deciding *whom* you will please with your work and service.

## Joseph as Able to See the Hand of God Working Things Out

> *Now therefore be not grieved, nor angry with yourselves, that ye sold me hither: for God did send me before you to preserve life.*
> GENESIS 45:5

> *But as for you, ye thought evil against me; but God meant it unto good, to bring to pass, as it is this day, to save much people alive.* GENESIS 50:20

To be spiritually-minded gives life and peace. To be carnally minded brings destruction. It is important that your mind works in a spiritual way. You must see the spiritual dimensions of everything that happens to you.

There are four ways to see things:

1. To see things in a completely natural way with no spiritual dimensions nor implications to anything.
2. To be conscious of the devil and see the devil at work in almost everything.

3. To blame God for all the bad experiences of your life.
4. To see the mysterious hand of God working things out as a father would for his child.

Joseph decided to accept the bad things that had been done to him as the hand of God working things out for his good. He believed that God had never left him in all his troubles. He believed that all the evils that were done to him by his wicked brothers were the hand of God at work and not the hand of the devil. He believed that nothing happened by chance. It was this understanding that gave him the ability to love his brothers and carry out God's plan to the fullest.

If he had seen his brothers as the cause of his calamities he would have tortured them with the slowest and most painful method available at the time. Recognising the hand of God as the reason for things helps you to forgive and not to blame anyone, not even yourself.

The art of following Joseph is the art of having this kind of understanding. The famous Scripturem -- "All things work together for good to them that love God and to them who are called according to his purpose" -- is a New Testament version of Joseph's philosophy. All great spiritual men who walked with God had this understanding.

Isaiah saw the hand of God at work when righteous people were taken away in death. He declared that they had been taken away to protect them from some evils ahead. He said, "The righteous perisheth, and no man layeth *it* to heart: and merciful men *are* taken away, none considering that the righteous is taken away from the evil *to come.* He shall enter into peace: they shall rest in their beds, *each one* walking *in* his uprightness" (Isaiah 57:1-2).

Paul saw the hand of God at work when Satan attacked him. He was under pressure; he was distressed, confused, in need and weakened. But he said, "And lest I should be exalted above measure through the abundance of the revelations, there was given to me a thorn in the flesh, the messenger of Satan to buffet me, lest I should be exalted above measure. For this thing I besought the Lord thrice, that it might depart from me. And he said unto me, "My grace is sufficient for thee: for my strength is made perfect in weakness. Most gladly therefore will I rather glory in my infirmities, that the power of Christ may rest upon me. Therefore I take pleasure in infirmities, in reproaches, in necessities, in persecutions, in distresses for Christ's sake: for when I am weak, then am I strong" (2 Corinthians 12:7-10).

Jesus knew that God His Father would never leave Him. When Pilate threatened Him with death and crucifixion, Jesus calmly explained to the arrogant Roman soldier that he *could and would have no power over Him unless God allowed it.*

> *And went again into the judgment hall, and saith unto Jesus, "Whence art thou?" But Jesus gave him no answer.*
>
> *Then saith Pilate unto him, "Speakest thou not unto me? Knowest thou not that I have power to crucify thee, and have power to release thee?"*
>
> *Jesus answered, "Thou couldest have no power at all against me, except it were given thee from above: therefore he that delivered me unto thee hath the greater sin."*
>
> *And from thenceforth Pilate sought to release him.*
> JOHN 19:9-12

## Joseph Believed There Can Be a Lean Season

> *Behold, there come seven ears of great plenty throughout all the land of Egypt:*
>
> *And there shall arise after them seven years of famine; and all the plenty shall be forgotten in the land of Egypt; and the famine shall consume the land.* GENESIS 41:29-30

The abundance of a good season can render deceptions and delusions to those who enjoy it. This is what the Bible calls the deceitfulness of riches. Riches come along with many deceptions. When there is abundance, it is difficult to believe that there can be a lean season. This is the reason why many rich people eventually become poor. The belief that life is in seasons is simply not there. Good seasons are so good that you just can't imagine that there can be a season so lean that it will make you forget your days of abundance.

I remember a brother who was enjoying a very good season of his life. It was so good that he boasted about his riches and abundance. He spent money recklessly and arrogantly. One day, while praying for him, I had a vision. In the vision, I saw the end of his abundance and the corrupting of his prosperity. The season of ill-favoured cows was about to descend on him but he could not perceive its possibility. When I warned him about it he brushed me away saying he was more than prepared for all eventualities. I could only watch helplessly as the vision was fulfilled.

The ability to *believe in the possibility* of such a season is what I am talking about here. Is it possible? Yes! Could it ever happen? Sure! Has it happened to anyone before? Affirmative! Is it likely to happen in my lifetime? Of course! Do people ever lose their wonderful jobs? Certainly! Do people ever have to leave the country in which they live today? You bet! Do people ever lose the favour they once had? Absolutely! Do people's circumstances ever change? Yup! Can there be a worldwide financial downturn? You better believe it.

The financial crises of the world basically affect those who do not have these beliefs. When you believe in the reality of lean seasons, you will be a much wiser person. You will be like Joseph who believed in the possibility of seven evil lean years. This conviction will lead you to live your life in a different way from someone who has no such beliefs.

## Joseph Prepared for the Future

> *LET PHARAOH DO THIS, and let him appoint officers over the land, and take up the fifth part of the land of Egypt in the seven plenteous years.*
>
> *And let them gather all the food of those good years that come, and lay up corn under the hand of Pharaoh, and let them keep food in the cities.*

> *And that food shall be for store to the land against the seven years of famine, which shall be in the land of Egypt; that the land perish not through the famine.* GENESIS 41:33-36

Preparing for the future is quite different from knowing and believing in the possibility of a bad season. There are many people who know and believe that there is going to be a bad season. It takes extra faith and energy to live with the future in mind.

It is so much easier to just enjoy the blessings of today! Why spend money on a problem that has not yet shown its head? Why spend money on something that looks so remote, so far fetched and so unlikely?

This ability to prepare for the future is what distinguishes the rich and the poor. Rich nations of the world are constantly preparing for remote and unlikely events. Before the Second World War, Germany re-armed itself and prepared extensively for war. Neighbouring countries could not comprehend the extent of destruction that was about to be unleashed on them. Millions of people next door in Poland were about to be slaughtered by Hitler's murderous war machine – the Wehrmacht. Yet, Poland made little preparation for the future. Even after Hitler had invaded Austria, they still seemed to have hope that the future would not be war. The price they paid was millions of lives.

Today, countries like Switzerland have laws in place, forcing everyone building a new house to construct a bomb shelter. These expensive bomb shelters are preparations they are making for a possible nuclear war. It may sound far-fetched but this is the art of preparation in practice.

As you read this book, God is showing you things in the future. He is giving you wisdom and grace to prepare for the future. Remember, it is not enough to know about it. What are you doing to prepare yourself for future difficulties and future lean seasons?

## Joseph Showed Love When He Became a Man of Authority

> *And when Joseph's brethren saw that their father was dead, they said, "Joseph will peradventure hate us, and will certainly*

*requite us all the evil which we did unto him." And they sent a messenger unto Joseph, saying, "Thy father did command before he died, saying,*

*'So shall ye say unto Joseph, Forgive, I pray thee now, the trespass of thy brethren, and their sin; for they did unto thee evil: and now, we pray thee, forgive the trespass of the servants of the God of thy father. And Joseph wept when they spake unto him.'"*

*And his brethren also went and fell down before his face; and they said, "Behold, we be thy servants."*

*And Joseph said unto them, "Fear not: for am I in the place of God?*

*But as for you, ye thought evil against me; but God meant it unto good, to bring to pass, as it is this day, to save much people alive.*

*Now therefore fear ye not: I will nourish you, and your little ones." And he comforted them, and spake kindly unto them.*
GENESIS 50:15-21

God took Joseph through a journey that softened and mellowed him. When he was mature and full of love, he was elevated into a place of authority. When a wicked person comes into a place of authority, much evil is released.

*When the righteous increase, the people rejoice, but when a wicked man rules, people groan.* PROVERBS 29:2 (NASB)

When people are in power, they usually go one of three ways. They forget how they used to be, they become more wicked or they become kinder. You must choose to become a kinder person who remembers all his struggles. You must choose to become someone who remembers his own problems and weaknesses. You must choose to become someone who sees God's hand at work. When you have this attitude you are ready to become a man or woman of authority.

## Joseph Did Things with Death and Eternity in Mind

*By faith Joseph, when he died, made mention of the departing of the children of Israel; and GAVE COMMANDMENT CONCERNING HIS BONES.* Hebrews 11:22

Joseph gave instructions with death in mind. He accepted the reality of his future. He knew that he would become a mere bag of bones and he gave instructions with that in mind. Few people do things with death and eternity in mind. Being conscious of death and of eternity induces the highest kind of wisdom in a person. Christians who have death in mind will live their lives seeking for rewards in heaven rather than building everything on earth.

Paul was conscious of death. He said, "I am in a strait betwixt two -- confused about whether to stay here or to go to heaven." On another occasion he said, "For me to live is Christ and to die is gain."

Jesus also had death and eternity in mind. He said, "I go to prepare a place for you." Surprisingly, death consciousness is the pivot around which true wisdom evolves and develops. Solomon was a bit late in becoming death conscious. He lived his life by concentrating on earthly things and earthly achievements. In the end, he was forced to say that all is vanity.

### The Wisdom of Death Consciousness

Death consciousness has a way of making you wiser, richer and smarter.

- A pastor who has death in mind will train young people and place them properly, so that the church will live beyond his life.
- A businessman who has death in mind will have deputies and successors in place, knowing that he may not be there to continue.
- A husband who has death in mind will be nice to his wife, knowing that she may not be there tomorrow.
- A wife who has death in mind will treat her husband with kindness knowing that he may be gone one day and she will miss him very much.
- Children who have death in mind will honor their parents and love them, knowing that their whole lives would change dramatically if

their parents were dead.

- Homeowners who have death in mind will write their wills clearly, knowing that they could suddenly not exist on this earth.

To follow Joseph you must focus on the reality of death and give commandments about when you returned to dust!

CHAPTER 10

# The Art of Following Moses

### Moses Genuinely Had No Confidence in Himself

*And Moses said unto God, "WHO AM I, that I should go unto Pharaoh, and that I should bring forth the children of Israel out of Egypt?"* EXODUS 3:11

*For we are the circumcision, which worship God in the spirit, and rejoice in Christ Jesus, and have no confidence in the flesh.* PHILIPPIANS 3:3

When Moses was offered a job in the ministry, his response was, "Who am I?" This response revealed his humility, his brokenness and his lack of confidence in himself. This tremendous spiritual quality had been worked in him by forty years of suffering in the wilderness of life and ministry. It was an important spiritual place that God had brought him to.

Often, God will lead you through journeys that force you to be humble. Many of life's experiences are orchestrated by the Holy Spirit to bring you to your knees and to make you humble. These are not my ideas. Read it for yourself: "And thou shalt remember all the way which the Lord thy God led thee these forty years in the wilderness, to humble thee, and to prove thee, to know what was in thine heart, whether thou wouldest keep his commandments, or no" (Deuteronomy 8:2).

Often, people are offered jobs in the ministry. Sometimes they are asked, "How do you feel about it?" People's responses are usually revealing. Some people say, "It's not a problem. I can do it." Others say, "I don't think I have the ability to do it." Although one response may sound more confident, it usually reveals arrogance towards the work of God.

Many such people think they are qualified, and perhaps even over-qualified. I have found that people who are not too confident about their abilities are usually more qualified spiritually to do the job. To think that you have anything to offer or that you are more than able to do God's work is usually a sign that you are the wrong person.

### The Paradox

There are two unusual and paradoxical attitudes that you will discover:

**A. Many spiritual people do not condemn sinners, neither are they surprised at the sins of people.**

Jesus did not condemn the woman caught in adultery. Neither did He seem surprised at her lewdness. Similarly, many doctors are not surprised at the things they see because they are used to seeing the human body with all its strange diseases. An experienced policeman is not surprised at the crimes of human beings. He is used to the wickedness and the lies of human nature.

**B. Spiritual people are highly conscious and genuinely ashamed of themselves and of their sinfulness.**

> *O wretched man that I am! Who shall deliver me from the body of this death?* ROMANS 7:24

Notice how Daniel confessed his sins, how the apostle Paul called himself the greatest of sinners and how Isaiah said, "Woe is me I am undone when he recognized his sinfulness. Peter knelt before Jesus saying, "Depart from me; for I am a sinful man." These spiritual giants acknowledged their wretchedness in such a disarming way that you know they are not just trying to sound or look humble.

## Moses Chose to Suffer Affliction

> *By faith Moses, when he was come to years, refused to be called the son of Pharaoh's daughter; choosing rather to suffer affliction with the people of God, than to enjoy the pleasures of sin for a season;* HEBREWS 11:24-25

Today, many Christians do not want to suffer any affliction. This concept comes from the type of preaching that we have. With church conference themes such as, "There Shall Be a Performance," " With God, All Things Are Possible," and "Our Year of Plenty," believers easily become primed to see a performance of God making them rich and to feel like there is never a need to suffer any kind of loss.

Because of not wanting to suffer anything at all, marriages are condemned to fail before they even start. In real life there is a lot of suffering in marriage. You cannot get into marriage without expecting to suffer in the end. You will be doomed to fail. The art of following Moses is the art of choosing and accepting to suffer and go through whatever God has decided for you. You must include suffering in your system of beliefs.

> *For unto you it is given in the behalf of Christ, not only to believe on him, but also to suffer for his sake* PHILIPPIANS 1:29

## Moses Did Not Enjoy the Pleasures of Sin

> *By faith Moses, when he was come to years, refused to be called the son of Pharaoh's daughter; choosing rather to suffer affliction with the people of God, than to enjoy the pleasures of sin for a season.* HEBREWS 11:24-25

To be successful, you will have to follow Moses in forsaking pleasures. Christianity is a religion of denying yourself, taking up your cross and following Christ. This means that there will be physical pleasures to forgo. Many Christians cannot imagine living without certain pleasures. That is why the numbers of missionaries going to poor parts of the world has become greatly reduced.

It is these little pleasures that the modern Christian is unwilling to part with. Being unwilling to part with little pleasures has sentenced many to hell. Millions have gone into damnation having no Saviour, having no salvation and having no hope.

In Africa, the incidence and level of infection of HIV is the same in the church as it is in the world. Why is this? It is because Christians have virtually the same lifestyle as unbelievers when it comes to their sexual lives. Modern Christians will not forsake the pleasures of sin for a season. The refusal to put away the pleasures of sin has brought about impurity, confusion and curses into the church. The art of following Moses is the art of putting away the pleasures of sin for a season.

## Moses Saw the Invisible

> *By faith he forsook Egypt, not fearing the wrath of the king: for he endured, as seeing him who is invisible.* HEBREWS 11:27

Compare a Christian who sees the invisible and one who does not. Believers whose hearts are set on the visible earthly treasures have a very different focus and ministry from those whose eyes are fixed on the invisible world.

### Pansy Christians

Pansy is a word I learned from some American friends. A pansy man is a weak, effeminate and often cowardly man. Our modern earthly-minded version of Christianity has produced pansy Christians who are unwilling to fight for the name of Jesus to be glorified. Pansy Christians fill the pews of the mega churches. Pansy pastors ridicule and insult bold ministers who take a strong stance against them, and constantly desecrate our Bibles, our Christ and what He stands for.

This state of affairs is created by a ministry that has kept its eyes and heart on earthly and visible goals. It is time to see angels. It is time to see Almighty God on His throne. It is time to see Jesus in all His glory. It is time to detect and to see the evil spirits, principalities and territorial spirits that dominate and influence people. Like Moses, seeing the invisible will transform you into a spiritual giant. Imagine that! Changed from being a pansy Christian into a mighty man or woman of valour!

## Moses Was Not Impressed by the World

> *By faith Moses, when he was come to years, refused to be called the son of Pharaoh's daughter;*
>
> *Choosing rather to suffer affliction with the people of God, than to enjoy the pleasures of sin for a season;*
>
> *Esteeming the reproach of Christ greater riches than the treasures in Egypt: for he had respect unto the recompence of the reward.*
> HEBREWS 11:24-26

Many of us are impressed with the world, with riches, with impressive buildings, shops, homes and fancy lives. But none of these things impressed Moses. He had been in Pharaoh's house for years but was not impressed by the life of an Egyptian king. He did not see anything in it that made it worth staying there. Unfortunately this cannot be said of many believers today.

One visit to America is enough to convince most African pastors to leave their poor African cities and migrate to America where they see an abundance of supermarkets, shiny lights, flashy cars, excellent roads and bridges. They are overwhelmed with the abundance of shopping malls, shoe shops, clothes shops and designer outlets. Somehow Moses was not impressed with the things he saw in the palace. He remained faithful to his Israeli heritage and calling.

Unfortunately, countless pastors have abandoned their calling in African nations for a more lucrative and profitable ministry in America. But there are not many pastors who abandoned America for the poor African cities. If we are going to achieve the great things that Moses did, we cannot afford to be impressed by Pharaoh's delicacies and delights. Decide not to be impressed by anything the world has to offer. You can live without it and be happy without any of these things.

## Moses Recognised the Role of Spiritual Counsellors

> *So Moses hearkened to the voice of his father-in-law, and did all that he had said.* EXODUS 18:24

Although Jethro was only a father-in-law to Moses, Moses submitted himself to his counsel. By this simple act, Moses revealed the importance of relating to different types of spiritual mentors and leaders. If Moses, the father of Israel, would submit himself to his father-in-law's counsel, do you not think that *you* should submit yourself to the pastors, counsellors and spiritual leaders in your life?

# CHAPTER 11

# The Art of Following Joshua

### Joshua Was a Can-Do Man

*And JOSHUA the son of Nun, and CALEB the son of Jephunneh, which were of them that searched the land, rent their clothes:*

*And THEY SPAKE unto all the company of the children of Israel, saying, "The land, which we passed through to search it, is an exceeding good land.*

*If the Lord delight in us, then he will bring us into this land, and give it us; a land which floweth with milk and honey.*

*Only rebel not ye against the Lord, neither fear ye the people of the land; for they are bread for us: their defence is departed from them, and the Lord is with us: fear them not."*

NUMBERS 14:6-9

Joshua is most remembered for being positive about Moses' plans to invade Jericho. The children of Israel are famous for being negative about these very same plans. It is Joshua's positive attitude that earned him a place in history and that got him delivered from the diseases that killed over one million other Israelites.

God listens to your words. Your words are a reflection of what is in your heart. Negative words are a reflection of a negative and rebellious attitude. There are people who are possessed with a spirit of opposition, reversal and rejection of every good purpose. This evil spirit is revealed through their words as they oppose the great plans and purposes of God!

The art of following Joshua is the art of becoming a positive person who believes things can be done. If you want to find people who do not have a can-do spirit, all you need is to attend a meeting and watch people's reactions as new ideas are introduced.

- "This can't be done."
- "It is not possible."
- "It may rain."
- "People don't like such things."
- "We don't have enough money."
- "It has not been done before."
- "So-and-so doesn't do it that way."

These are a few common responses you can expect from people who do not have a can-do spirit. The fact that you are even reading this book shows that you have a can-do attitude. Open your heart and believe that God can and will do greater things through your life. Reject the influences of people in your life who do not have a can-do attitude.

**The Seven Can-Do Statements of Joshua**

1. The land is an exceedingly good land.
2. If the Lord delights in us, He will bring us into this land.
3. If the Lord delights in us, He will give us the land.
4. The land of Canaan is a land flowing with milk and honey.
5. Do not be afraid of the people of the land.
6. The people are bread for us.
7. The people no longer have a defence.

## Joshua Developed an Independent Mind and Did Not Need to Follow the Crowd

*Your carcases shall fall in this wilderness; and ALL THAT WERE NUMBERED OF YOU, according to your whole number, from twenty years old and upward, which have murmured against me,*

*Doubtless ye shall not come into the land, concerning which I sware to make you dwell therein, SAVE CALEB THE SON OF JEPHUNNEH, AND JOSHUA THE SON OF NUN.*

Numbers 14:29-30

Most people depend on the feelings and emotions of the crowd. "Who else is doing it?" they asked. Am I the only one? Who else passed and who else failed are the common questions asked when exam results are released. There is so much comfort in being part of a group. Your ability to have an independent mind that does not have to tow the line of the majority or the crowd is a sign that you are a man or woman of conviction.

Jesus recommended John the Baptist because he was this kind of person. He was a not a reed that would sway and bend with the flow of the wind. He would stand up for what he believed and declare it boldly. He was even prepared to die for what he believed.

This is what Joshua did when he declared a contrary opinion in the presence of two million angry and rebellious Israelis (the majority). The majority is certainly not always right! The choices that the majority makes during some elections are the clearest evidence that the majority is often wrong.

## Joshua Was Not Drawn into the Culture of Murmuring and Complaining

*And the Lord spake unto Moses and unto Aaron, saying, "How long shall I bear with this evil congregation, which murmur against me? I have heard the murmurings of the children of*

*Israel, which they murmur against me."* NUMBERS 14:26-27

Murmuring and complaining can become the culture of any office, church or group. The Israelites developed this culture of being dissatisfied, discontent and disenchanted by everything their leader did. They complained about everything until their complaints sounded like madness.

Complaining and murmuring is satanic in its very nature. Demonic things often make no sense when they are analysed. It does not make sense when people shout and rave for being delivered from slavery. The senseless and unreasonable outbursts of the Israelites revealed the presence of demons amongst them.

Has your church developed a culture of whispering, commenting, murmuring and discussing, analysing, criticising anything and everything? If that is what has happened in your church, you need to get out as soon as possible. You are sitting on a spiritual time bomb. Destruction is marked out for all who complain and murmur.

**Miriam developed leprosy because she murmured against Moses. The Israelites developed plagues and diseases when they murmured against the Lord.**

> *And the men, which Moses sent to search the land, who returned, and made all the congregation to murmur against him, by bringing up a slander upon the land,*
>
> *Even those men that did bring up the evil report upon the land, died by the plague before the Lord.*
>
> *But Joshua the son of Nun, and Caleb the son of Jephunneh, which were of the men that went to search the land, lived still.*
> NUMBERS 14:36-38

## Joshua was Able to Stay Close to a Great Man of God Without Being Offended

*And blessed is he, whosoever shall not be offended in me.*
LUKE 7:23

The Greek word "offended" is *skandalizo.* (Where does it come from?) It means to *see in someone something you disapprove of* and *something that incurs your displeasure.* Some people always see something they disapprove of. Somehow, you must develop the art of staying close to a man of God without *seeing* something you disapprove of.

How come your eyes are always seeing the negative? How come you always notice something that you disapprove of? Offense (Skandalizo) puts you in the place where you cannot receive from a person.

Joshua was a personal servant of Moses. He must have known him very well because of the personal work he was involved with. Yet he did not develop any airs or negative attitudes towards Moses. "And Moses rose up, and his minister Joshua: and Moses went up into the mount of God" (Exodus 24:13).

Moses laid hands on Joshua and he received wisdom to lead the people. Amazingly, Aaron, Moses' brother and assistant was not chosen to succeed Moses. Instead, Joshua the menial servant was chosen to be the successor of Moses.

## Joshua Had the Ability to Step into the Shoes of a Great Man of God

> *Now it came about after the death of Moses the servant of the Lord that the Lord spoke to Joshua the son of Nun, Moses' servant, saying,*
>
> *"Moses My servant is dead; now therefore arise, cross this Jordan, you and all this people, to the land which I am giving to them, to the sons of Israel."* JOSHUA 1:1-2 (NASB)

> *And Joshua the son of Nun was full of the spirit of wisdom; for Moses had laid his hands upon him: and the children of Israel hearkened unto him, and did as the Lord commanded Moses.*
> DEUTERONOMY 34:9

Joshua inherited the nation Israel and did a great job of moving things forward. He inherited a struggling nation in the wilderness but took them across the river Jordan and into the Promised Land. He divided up the Promised Land for the people of Israel and left them in a vastly improved condition. This is what must happen when you are called upon to step into the shoes of a great person, such as a wise parent or relative, a leader in your company or workplace, or another mentor or counsellor in your life.

Sadly, I must report that only two percent of people who inherit wealth are able to increase it. It is much easier to inherit money than it is to inherit the attitudes and the principles that created that wealth. Because of a failure to learn from the principles, those who inherit wealth often lose it all. You can only step into a great person's shoes if you study and understand what he or she did.

**Four Keys to Stepping into a Great Person's Shoes**

**1. Humility:**

Rehoboam stepped into his father's shoes with a prideful attitude and lost ninety percent of what his father had worked for. All great people were helped by others to become who they were. You will have to respect all those helpers and the contributions they made. Failing to respect them will make you fail abysmally.

You have to stay humble when you step into a great person's shoes because pride will blind you to the reasons for his success. Pride will also make you despise a great person for his mistakes.

**2. Admiration for the great person you are replacing:**

It is this admiration that will make you realise that the great person ahead of you knew something that you don't. It will also make you realise that the person understood some things that you do not. Admiration opens your heart and makes you a receiver.

The reason why people work for wealthy people and remain poor is because they despise and even hate them. You cannot learn from someone you despise dislike! You can only learn from somebody you admire!

**3. Learning what the great person you are replacing knew:**

Knowledge is the foundation on which people build things. If you do not know what a doctor knows, you cannot become a doctor. You have to know all the laws and principles a lawyer knows to become a lawyer. It is important to at least acquire the knowledge that your predecessor had.

**4. Understanding the person you are replacing:**

You may know what your predecessor knew, but you may not know why he did or did not do certain things. Gaining a better understanding of why things are done the way they are done is what will enable you step into a great person's shoes.

## Joshua Was Bold and Courageous

> *Be strong and of a GOOD COURAGE: for unto this people shalt thou divide for an inheritance the land, which I sware unto their fathers to give them.*
>
> *Only be thou STRONG AND VERY COURAGEOUS, that thou mayest observe to do according to all the law, which Moses my servant commanded thee: turn not from it to the right hand or to the left, that thou mayest prosper whithersoever thou goest.*
>
> JOSHUA 1:6-7

Good courage is what Joshua needed to accomplish his ministry. Good courage is also called boldness and boldness is what you need to move into new territory in your Christian walk! *You do not need boldness to stay at home. But you need a lot of boldness to venture into new ground.*

Joshua's secret was to enter new territory. He ventured out into the Promised Land. He stepped into new and dangerous things that he had never encountered or handled before. Everything God has planned for you will require boldness.

When I started a church in 1987, I needed boldness. When I ventured out into the healing ministry I needed even more boldness to pray for the sick. You cannot manufacture healings; you cannot shout them into existence. There are either miracles or no miracles.

Indeed, boldness is a key to the power of God.

## Joshua Learned to Meditate on the Word of God

> *This book of the law shall not depart out of thy mouth; but thou shalt MEDITATE THEREIN DAY AND NIGHT, that thou mayest observe to do according to all that is written therein: for then thou shalt make thy way prosperous, and then thou shalt have good success.* JOSHUA 1:8

There is a difference between reading and meditation. Most people do not read books. Out of those who read, just a few meditate carefully on what they read. What does this leave us with? Very, very few people actually meditate on the Word of God or on what they read! Where does this leave us? It leaves us with very, very few really successful people.

Meditation is a key to success in school, in university and in life. It is those who meditate on the Word who really understand what they read. Meditation on the Word of God was a key to the success of Joshua. Following Joshua will require you to faithfully meditate on the Word of God. You can always tell when you meet someone who meditates on the Word of God. He is full of insight and revelation of the things he reads. He teaches you the scriptures you already know and you wonder if you have read them before!

When you meditate on something, you understand it in a very different way. That is when it begins to benefit you. Meditation is the key you need for your life and ministry. It is the key that will make you like Joshua and cause you to enter new territories.

I have spent years sharing with people the books I have discovered. Very few of those who hear me actually meditate on the books I find so precious. Very few ministers really meditate on what the apostles, prophets and teachers have written. That is why it does not benefit them the way it could.

# CHAPTER 12

# The Art of Following King David

## David Did Not Despise Small Things

*And Eliab his eldest brother heard when he spake unto the men; and Eliab's anger was kindled against David, and he said, Why camest thou down hither? and with WHOM HAST THOU LEFT THOSE FEW SHEEP in the wilderness?...*
1 Samuel 17:28

Do not be afraid of small beginnings; God will lift you up. David was handling a few sheep, but he benefited greatly from those small, early experiences. It was while looking after a small flock that he had a fight with a bear and a lion. From facing those impossible situations he was able to take on Goliath.

**Don't Rush Success**

Why are you in such a hurry to be successful? If you make a mistake with a hundred dollars, it will be easier for you to recover than if you make that same mistake with a hundred thousand dollars. Any businessman who is able to succeed with a small amount of money can succeed with a larger amount of money. *Smallness is a necessary stage in the kingdom of God.* It is a necessary stage for every business executive. It humbles you and makes you trust in God.

**Jesus taught us three principles of progress:**

- The principle of being faithful with small things (Luke 16:10).
- The principle of being faithful with another man's things (Luke 16:12).
- The principle of being faithful with money (Luke 16:11).

You cannot circumvent any one of these laws. Start small and harden your forehead. Avoid people who would laugh at you and despise you. Stay with those who believe in you. Do not tell people what you are doing if they do not respect you. You can make it! God is on your side! God is with you! The Greater One is with you and in you!

Do not run away from small beginnings. They are God's training ground for you. That is how King David got his education -- in the school of small beginnings!

## David Embraced Menial Jobs

> *And David came to Saul, and stood before him: and he loved him greatly; and he became his ARMOURBEARER.*
> 1 Samuel 16:21

When studying the life of David, you soon learn that though he became king, he first performed many menial jobs. In his father's house, he was a shepherd. While at the king's palace, he did the work of a musician, servant, errand boy and armour-bearer. He wasn't even a soldier! There are so many Christians who want to start out on top! But the only job that begins at the top is grave digging!

If you study the background of many great people, you will discover that most of them once served at the lowest level in their profession. I have done nearly every kind of menial job in the church. I was a drummer, organist, cleaner and odd-job man. All these have helped me to be a better leader. Do not shy away from menial jobs.

## David Ministered to Others

> *And it came to pass, when the evil spirit from God was upon Saul, that DAVID TOOK AN HARP, AND PLAYED WITH HIS HAND: SO SAUL WAS REFRESHED, and was well, and the evil spirit departed from him.* 1 SAMUEL 16:23

If you want to be successful in this life, decide to be a blessing to others. This will unlock the gates for blessings to flow into your life.

*The most successful people in the world have often played a vital role in someone else's life.* Perhaps they were doctors who saved the sick. Maybe they were pastors who ministered to the needs of the people. Perhaps they produced something that benefited millions of people.

David took advantage of the opportunity to minister to Saul. Whenever evil spirits came to torment Saul, David refreshed him by playing the harp and singing unto the Lord. He suddenly became useful to Saul and his kingdom. Are you useful to anyone? **Your value rises with your usefulness!**

There are some Christians who just say, "Give me, give me, give me." When are you going to start giving something? When are you going to be a blessing to somebody? Jesus is so valuable to all of us because He saved our souls by giving His life.

David's value rapidly increased after he helped Saul in his time of demonic affliction. Take up your opportunity of counselling and helping people and sharing the Word of God. Take up the responsibility of ministering to others. I notice how people shy away from doing God's work. They feel it will be a bother. They feel it will keep them away from succeeding in their secular field. What a mistake! They don't realise that as they help others, they become more valuable to society. The more valuable you are, the more important you will be.

## David Knew That Not Everyone Would Accept Him

### Avoid People Who Despise You

> *...Eliab's anger was kindled against david, and he said, Why camest thou down hither? and with whom hast thou left those few sheep in the wilderness? I know thy pride, and the naughtiness of thine heart; for thou art come down that thou mightest see the battle. And David said, What have I now done? Is there not a cause? And HE TURNED FROM HIM TOWARD ANOTHER...* 1 Samuel 17:28-30

This scripture describes the persecution David faced from his brothers. Eliab, obviously intimidated by David, hurled insults at him just when he was about to fight with Goliath. The world has two types of people: those who believe in you and those who have no confidence in you. Learn to turn away from people who despise you.

I once spoke to a doctor who was living abroad. I told him, "You have never believed in me. When we were medical students in Accra, you despised me." He answered, "How did you know? What you are saying is true." He continued, "Somehow in those days, I didn't like what you were doing. But now, I have come to appreciate your ministry."

I had always known that this fellow despised me. Though he never said much to me, I knew it in my spirit. Just like David, I turned away from him and "flowed" with those who believed in me. No one can flourish in an environment of despisement.

In some churches, lay people are thought of as being incapable of ministry work. In some places, poor and uneducated people are despised. It is important to turn away from an environment where you are despised. You can only flourish where people respect and love you.

### David Avoided People Who Were Jealous of Him

> *And the evil spirit from the Lord was upon Saul, as he sat in his house with his javelin in his hand: and David played with his hand. And Saul sought to smite David even to the wall with the javelin; but he slipped away out of Saul's presence, and*

> *he smote the javelin into the wall: and DAVID FLED, AND ESCAPED that night.* 1 SAMUEL 19:9-10

Anyone whom God has blessed will begin to have arrows of hatred and jealousy thrown at him. You may do good and only good, but you will be hated because of your success. This is part of life. It is your duty to avoid the arrows of hatred.

**Avoid People who Hate You**

When you see one arrow of Satan, you should know that there are many more out there primed to destroy you. If you sit in the same place, the next arrow will get you. There are times when it is wiser to run away than to stand and fight. One time, the Pharisees wanted to kill Jesus. When Jesus learned of this, He withdrew Himself from that area.

"Then the Pharisees went out, and held a council against him, how they might destroy him. But WHEN JESUS KNEW IT, HE WITHDREW HIMSELF from thence" (Matthew 12:14, 15),

Young Christian men must know that they attract the arrows of Satan because of the gift of God in their lives. In fact, the Bible teaches that because of the anointing on your life, young ladies will be attracted to you.

> *Because of the savour of thy good ointments [anointing] thy name is as OINTMENT [anointing] poured forth, therefore do THE VIRGINS LOVE THEE.* SONGS OF SOLOMON 1:3

Young lady, because you are beautiful, many wicked and adulterous men are interested in you. Run away from those arrows immediately, otherwise, your whole life may be destroyed. The Bible teaches that precious ministers are sought for by the devil. Anyone who is a precious instrument of God will be hunted after!

For by means of a whorish woman a man is brought to a piece of bread: and THE ADULTERESS WILL HUNT FOR THE PRECIOUS LIFE (Proverbs 6:26).

Years ago, some sisters were interested in me because of my gift. I didn't even know the danger I was in. Many sisters in Christ I ministered to were hearing wedding bells in addition to the Word of God. I would go around from house to house and room to room sharing the Word of God. Little did I know that some sisters were falling in love with me because of the anointing.

One day, the Lord instructed me to choose a wife. All along, I had been saying, "I will not marry for at least ten more years." But the Lord spoke to me and said, "Your life is precious. You are walking in danger that you don't even know about." Choose your wife now and stay close to her.

## David Allowed God to Work Things Out

> *And David said to Abishai, DESTROY HIM NOT: for who can stretch forth his hand against the Lord's anointed, AND BE GUILTLESS? David said furthermore, As the Lord liveth, THE LORD SHALL SMITE HIM; or HIS DAY SHALL COME TO DIE; or HE SHALL DESCEND INTO BATTLE, AND PERISH.* 1 Samuel 26:9,10

In this passage, David reveals his inner thoughts. He said, "Even though King Saul is fighting against me, I will not kill him myself." David was not stupid! He knew that Saul had to die. However, he was not going to be the person to kill Saul.

He gave several options about how the prophecy concerning his kingship would happen. There was no way that David could become king as long as there was a king on the throne. David gave three options about how his dream of kingship and freedom could come to pass.

The first possibility was that the Lord would strike Saul down supernaturally. The second possibility was that Saul would eventually die naturally. David said, "His day shall come to die." The third possibility was that the king could be killed in a battle. It is interesting to note that the Lord worked out the plan for David's kingship through the third option. Saul was indeed killed in a battle. The point that I am making is that David did not get involved in the implementation of God's master plan. He left it to God and kept his hands clean!

Everyone could see that God was doing His own thing. We need to trust

God for His perfect plan to materialise. When you get involved and try to help God, you create Ishmaels who grow up to challenge your Isaacs.

> *And Moses said unto the people, Fear ye not, STAND STILL, AND SEE THE SALVATION OF THE LORD, which he will shew to you today: for the Egyptians whom ye have seen today, ye shall see them again no more forever. THE LORD SHALL FIGHT FOR YOU, and ye shall hold your peace.*
> EXODUS 14:13, 14

Pastors must know that if God wants certain people to be in their churches, there is no need to steal them from another congregation. Perhaps the Lord will bring them to your church through one circumstance or another. Just leave it to Him. Do not get involved in any unethical dealings with another pastor's church members.

If God wants you to marry that man, it will work out. Ladies, there is no need to throw yourself at a man for him to notice you.

After four years of marriage, one man told his wife, "You forced yourself on me! I never even had the chance to think about it properly." Perhaps this man would have found her anyway. But because she forced herself on him, he was wondering whether he made the right decision. It is time to allow God to work things out Himself. Keep your hands clean!

## David Didn't Accept What He Had Not Tested

> *And Saul armed David with his armour…And David said unto Saul, I CANNOT GO WITH THESE; FOR I HAVE NOT PROVED THEM. And David put them off him. And he took his staff in his hand, and chose him five smooth stones… and his sling was in his hand: and he drew near to the Philistine.* 1 SAMUEL 17:38-40

This was the turning point in David's ministry. He had an opportunity to have his greatest breakthrough - *it was a matter of do or die!* As he went forth, he was to make one of the most important decisions of his life: to wear Saul's armour or not. He decided against wearing Saul's armour and opted for his slingshot with just five smooth stones. In this act, you see the principle of choosing what you have tested.

**Marry the Person You Know!**

I marvel at the behaviour of certain Christian men. They behave normally up until the time they are about to get married. Instead of marrying someone whom they know, they go for a mysterious personality whom nobody knows. They choose a young lady who they know very little about. David refused to use Saul's armour because he hadn't tested it. How can you marry someone you hardly know?

Surely, there are some nice people in the church whom you can marry! It is important to marry someone who has a good reputation in the church.

**Your Slingshot Will Lead You to Victory**

If you really plan to win the battle against Goliath, don't use Saul's armour! That may be the prescribed and ordained method, but using that which is familiar to you will help you to be victorious! **Stay with the five smooth stones that have brought you victory in the past. If you use them in the day of your greatest challenge, you will prosper!**

I know many of my church members from my secondary school days. They've also known me throughout the years. Go for someone that you've known for a number of years. Choose someone whose character you can vouch for.

## David Was Flexible and Adaptable

Everything changes and the best way to protect yourself is to keep yourself adaptable and on-the-move. You must be as fluid and formless as water. Everything changes. Don't put your hopes on a lasting method or a lasting order. Instead of taking a form that your enemy can grasp, keep yourself fluid and flexible in the Master's hand.

> *And David said unto Ahimelech the priest, The king hath commanded me a business, and hath said unto me, Let no*

> *man know anything of the business whereabout I send thee, and what I have commanded thee... Now therefore what is under thine hand? GIVE ME FIVE LOAVES OF BREAD IN MINE HAND, OR WHAT THERE IS PRESENT.*
>
> 1 SAMUEL 21:2, 3

In the passage of Scripture above, you will realise that David acted like a *poor* man. In the Scripture quoted below, David pretended to be a *mad* man.

> *And David arose, and fled that day for fear of Saul, and went to Achish the king of Gath. And he changed his behaviour before them, and FEIGNED HIMSELF MAD in their hands, and scrabbled on the doors of the gate, AND LET HIS SPITTLE FALL DOWN UPON HIS BEARD.*
>
> 1 SAMUEL 21:10, 13

Was he really mad? No. He was the king's son-in-law. He was from a good family. He was certainly not out of his mind. However, for that occasion, David had to behave like a mad man in order to survive. I constantly marvel at how some Christians are unable to adapt in order to breakthrough in life. You may have to do without a car for a season so that you can have fewer bills to pay. You may have to live in a smaller apartment so that you can save some money.

It amazes me that when someone is successful, people hate him all the more. They call him names. They say that he is proud. But they never look closely enough to see what is making that person successful. The apostle Paul said, "I adapt to all men in order that I may win some people to Christ."

> *To the weak became I as weak...I AM MADE ALL THINGS TO ALL MEN, that I might by all means save some.*
>
> 1 CORINTHIANS 9:22

David adapted. Paul adapted. Why can't you adapt?

## David Behaved Wisely in His Season of Prosperity

> *And David BEHAVED HIMSELF WISELY in all his ways; and the Lord was with him. Wherefore when Saul saw that he BEHAVED HIMSELF VERY WISELY, he was afraid of him. Then the princes of the Philistines went forth: and it came to pass, after they went forth, that David BEHAVED HIMSELF MORE WISELY than all the servants of Saul; so that his name was much set by.* 1 SAMUEL 18:14, 15, 30

At different times of your life, God will bless you and lift you up. Many people think that problems belong to those who are poor and defeated. You will notice that David's problems did not begin until after he killed Goliath. After one breakthrough came a host of problems. But the Bible says that David behaved himself wisely. It is important to walk in wisdom when the Lord has promoted you.

Whenever I go to Takoradi, a city in Ghana, my wife points out some buildings to me; buildings which were inherited by a certain family. Although their father left them a lot of wealth and property, that family is now penniless and at the mercy of others. Although they inherited a lot of money, they did not benefit from it. Perhaps they did not know how to handle their newly found riches. They misused what they inherited until they had to sell all their properties to pay back their debts.

The problem is that many do not know how to behave themselves wisely when they are blessed. Some young ladies backslide as soon as they get married. They forget that God gave them their husband. They no longer attend prayer meetings and they want to stay away from the church. Never forget that the Lord gave you everything you have. Learn to behave wisely every time the Lord blesses you!

One Christian lady once told me of how she backslid after her marriage. She and her husband were serious Christians who used to be at every meeting. She told me, "It is my fault. At a point during our marriage, I stopped coming for prayer meetings with my husband." She told me how one night when she was lying in bed with her husband, he turned to her and said, "Is it not time for the all-night prayer meeting?" She told him,

"Oh, let's not bother tonight." She did that a few times until her husband stopped going to prayer meetings altogether.

Why do people fall away when God blesses them? Why do you have to stop going to prayer meetings just because you are married? It is time to know how to behave wisely after the breakthrough comes.

## David Avoided Isolation

> *But all Israel and Judah loved David, because HE WENT OUT AND CAME IN BEFORE THEM.* 1 SAMUEL 18:16

Unsuccessful people usually live solitary lives. Fellowship is a very important part of success. The more you interact with godly people, the more godliness will rub off onto you. The more you interact with successful people, the more successful you will become. But success also has a way of isolating you.

David did not isolate himself. He kept in touch and that helped him immensely. In fact, the Bible teaches us that this is a sign that you are a Christian. "We know that we have passed from death unto life, because WE LOVE THE BRETHREN. He that loveth not his brother abideth in death" (1 John 3:14).

If you are walking in the light, you will often be found fellowshipping with others.

> *But if we walk in the light, as he is in the light, WE HAVE FELLOWSHIP ONE WITH ANOTHER, and the blood of Jesus Christ his Son cleanseth us from all sin.* 1 JOHN 1:7

**11. (?) Where's 1-10? The art of following David is the art of recognizing the spiritual identity of everyone you meet.**

The Bible describes the antichrist as a beast who has particular characteristics. Even though the antchrist is actually a man, the Bible describes what he really is. He is a beast with seven heads and ten horns. On his heads are the names of blasphemies, insults and confusion. Spiritually speaking, the beast is like a leopard whose feet are like the feet of a bear and whose mouth is like the mouth of a lion. This grotesque creature I just described is from the book of Revelation so that you have a clearer understanding of what you are dealing with.

It is important to recognise everyone you are dealing with in a spiritual way. You may be dealing with a beast and not even know it. Knowing what you are dealing with will help you to fight it. Catching a leopard is very different from catching a lion. Leopards live in trees and behave like ghosts who are hardly ever seen. Lions walk about freely in the savanna.

> *And he said unto his men, The Lord forbid that I should do this thing unto MY MASTER, the Lord's anointed, to stretch forth mine hand against him, seeing he is the ANOINTED OF THE LORD. David also arose afterward, and went out of the cave, and cried after Saul, saying, MY LORD THE KING…Moreover, MY FATHER…* 1 Samuel 24:6,8,11

In this passage, David spoke about King Saul to his subordinates. What struck me about David's speech was the way he referred to the king. At one point, he called him, "*My lord.*" At other times, he called him, "*My king,*" "*My master,*" and even "*My father.*"

He could have called him a *demon-possessed* man. He could have referred to him as the *demoniac*. We all know that Saul had a problem with evil spirits. We all know that King Saul was a fallen man of God. Everyone knew that the anointing had departed. Yet, David gave Saul the honor and referred to him in a spiritual and honorable way.

Some people think that titles are not important. I think that titles have a role to play, especially in a big organization. Whatever you think about titles, one of the good things they do is that they help you to see with whom you are dealing. They help you to remember at all times who you are and who you are not!

Because David constantly reminded himself that he was dealing with the anointed king, it was difficult for him to strike the Lord's anointed. As you associate with a man of God, familiarity may make you forget whom you are with. David never forgot that Saul was his master. He never forgot that Saul was his father-in-law. And he did not allow himself to forget that he was dealing with an anointed man of God. This, I believe, was one of the secrets of David's success.

If David had killed Saul, it would have been because he felt justified to kill a demonized and fallen man of God. He would have thought that he was helping God to eliminate this disgraceful man. Of course, killing a raving lunatic is perceived as different from killing God's servant. However, David never allowed himself to see Saul as a madman. David's respect for Saul's office was maintained until the very end. When David heard of Saul's death, he spoke of him as the "mighty."

> *How are the MIGHTY fallen in the midst of the battle! O Jonathan thou wast slain in thine high places.* 2 SAMUEL 1:25

David went on and described Saul as the *beauty of Israel.*

> *THE BEAUTY OF ISRAEL is slain upon thy high places: how are the mighty fallen!* 2 SAMUEL 1:19

This is remarkable considering how Saul had deteriorated in life. I believe that years later, this act of seeing King Saul in the right way saved David's life.

David had taught his men that kings and other anointed people are not to be murdered. The unspoken message that came through David's actions was loud and clear. **Do not touch the Lord's anointed, no matter what!** Years later, when David himself made a mistake and killed Uriah, he opened the door for a possible retaliatory act. Uriah the Hittite was one of the mighty men of God. You will find him listed as the last of David's mighty warriors.

> *These be the names of THE MIGHTY MEN whom David had... URIAH THE HITTITE: thirty and seven in all.*
> 2 SAMUEL 23:8, 39

Since David had killed one of these mighty men, the other mighty men could have retaliated. They could have justified the murder of King David saying, "He's a fallen man of God." They could have said, "We know him. He's an adulterer and a murderer." But David had taught them by example, not to strike at the Lord's anointed.

In today's world, it is important to perceive the Lord's anointed as they truly are. It is important both in private and in public to refer to your pastor in a honorable way. If you call him "Joe Diggy" when you speak about him in private, that is what he will be to you.

If you refer to him as "my pastor," that is what he will be to you. You must realise that faith comes by hearing. What you hear yourself say repeatedly affects your faith. *Remember that God will often bless you through a man of God. God's method is to use men as channels and vessels of blessing.* Paul said, "Henceforth, know we no man after the flesh." In other words, I do not see people through the eyes of my flesh anymore.

> *Wherefore henceforth know we no man after the flesh: yea, though we have known Christ after the flesh, yet now henceforth know we him no more.* 2 CORINTHIANS 5:16

If you see someone as a friend, classmate or an equal, then that is what he or she will be to you. Learn to keep a spiritual perspective on the people you are dealing with. It will keep you on safe ground all the time.

## David Honored His Spiritual Leaders

> *And he said unto his men, THE LORD FORBID THAT I SHOULD DO THIS THING UNTO MY MASTER, the Lord's anointed, to stretch forth mine hand against him, seeing he is the anointed of the Lord.* 1 SAMUEL 24:6

Evil spirits try to cut off spiritual leaders from their "flock." One of the secrets of success is to honor both your natural and spiritual fathers, until the very end.

God knows that many fathers do not live up to standard. However, He expects a certain honor to flow from children to the fathers. Just accept it! The promise is clear: If you honor your father it will be well with you and you will live long on the surface of the earth.

> *HONOR THY FATHER and mother; which is the first commandment with promise; that IT MAY BE WELL WITH THEE, and THOU MAYEST LIVE LONG ON THE EARTH.* Ephesians 6:2, 3

*There are many fathers who can and do provoke their children greatly.* Children should be careful not to retaliate, even under extreme provocation.

> *And, ye fathers, PROVOKE NOT your children to wrath…*
> Ephesians 6:4

I have been provoked many times by fathers -- both natural and spiritual fathers. It has been one of my greatest commitments to honor these fathers in the midst of betrayal and direct attacks. It is not easy to honor some of them, but I believe that it leads to God's blessing and favour.

## David Took Advice Seriously

> *And David said to Abigail, Blessed be the Lord God of Israel, which sent thee this day to meet me: And BLESSED BE THY ADVICE, and blessed be thou, which hast kept me this day from coming to shed blood, and from avenging myself with mine own hand.* 1 Samuel 25:32, 33

In this Scripture, you see David about to make a mistake. He was going to attack innocent people. Nabal had been very ungrateful to David for his services. It was the advice of Abigail that saved the day. Once again, if King David had shed blood in his early days it could have become an embarrassment and a curse to him. This would have followed him throughout his reign as king.

David said to Abigail, "**Blessed be thy advice.**" Thank God for people who give good advice. Be open to their advice. *Even when your enemy is speaking, take note of what he is saying.* There are many people who advise me. I have lawyers, architects, engineers, doctors and businessmen who make great inputs into my life. I am the leader, so I have to make the decisions. However, I want to know what everybody thinks before I make the decision. Sometimes, even children can give you good advice.

There is a mystery about good advice. The one who is advising sees the issues very clearly and simply. Often, the one who is receiving the advice does not believe that things are as simple as that. Open your spirit to be able to see when good advice is coming your way.

**Receive Advice From Your Pastor**

"That the king said unto NATHAN THE PROPHET [his pastor], See now, I dwell in an house of cedar, but the ark of God dwelleth within curtains. And Nathan said to the king, Go, do all that is in thine heart; for the Lord is with thee. And it came to pass that night, that the word of the Lord came unto Nathan, saying, Go and tell my servant David, thus saith the Lord…" (2 Samuel 7:2-5)

David had a pastor. He had someone who could speak into his life spiritually. Having a pastor is different from belonging to a church. People may belong to a church but have no shepherd over their lives. Is there anyone who can speak into your life? There are many people in my church. I have found out that some of them want to receive counsel, while others do not. I do not just advise every Tom, Dick and Harry in the church. I speak to those who make it clear that they want the input.

David consulted his pastor, Nathan, when he wanted to build a temple. Nathan gave him good advice. Pastor Nathan later brought a specific word from the Lord concerning the temple. Later, when David fell into adultery, Pastor Nathan had the confidence to minister to the king. He knew that the king would not be offended. He knew that the king would receive it as the word of the Lord.

> *And the Lord sent Nathan unto David… And David's anger was greatly kindled against the man; and he said to Nathan, As the Lord liveth, the man that hath done this thing shall surely die... And Nathan said to David, THOU ART THE MAN… And DAVID SAID UNTO NATHAN, I HAVE SINNED AGAINST THE LORD. And Nathan said unto David, The Lord also hath put away thy sin; thou shalt not die.*
>
> 2 Samuel 12:1, 5, 7, 13

I know that there are some people in my church who are living in the wrong way. But I also realize that some of these people are not open to receive the pastor's counsel. I just preach and teach generally. If they make themselves open to a direct spiritual word from me, I will certainly tell them what the Word of God says. Everybody needs help, but not everybody wants help!

David could have reacted by arresting Nathan. He could have told Nathan that he was having bad dreams and becoming too suspicious. Jeremiah the prophet was arrested several times because of the prophetic word he gave.

> *Now Pashur the son of Immer the priest, who was also chief governor in the house of the Lord heard that Jeremiah prophesied these things. Then Pashur smote Jeremiah the prophet, and put him in the stocks...* JEREMIAH 20:1, 2

Your ability to receive certain rebukes from the Lord is seen by the way you handled the earlier word you received. David had already demonstrated that he would be obedient to the voice of the Lord. That is why his pastor was bold enough to speak to him.

## David Was Quick to See and Admit His Mistakes

It is interesting to note that God describes David as a man after His own heart. We all know that David was far from being perfect. Could it be that God was not looking for perfection?

What makes us great in God's sight is the manner in which we deal with our mistakes. Almost every person in the Bible made mistakes. From Adam to Peter, the Bible is replete with stories of impeachable offences. Yet, God has been merciful to His children.

When Saul made a mistake, he was confronted by the pastor of his day. Notice how Saul argued with the prophet Samuel. He insisted that he had not done anything wrong.

> *Wherefore then didst thou not obey the voice of the Lord, but didst fly upon the spoil, and didst evil in the sight of the Lord?*

> *And SAUL SAID unto Samuel, YEA I HAVE OBEYED THE VOICE OF THE LORD... And Samuel said...Behold, to obey is better than sacrifice...Because thou hast rejected the word of the Lord, he hath also rejected thee from being king.*
> 1 SAMUEL 15:19, 20, 22, 23

He argued that he had done the right thing. The evidence was there, yet he denied any wrongdoing. Compare this to David. When David was confronted by the pastor of his day (Nathan), he immediately said, "I have sinned." He admitted his wrongdoing, although no one could even have proved it.

> *Wherefore hast thou despised the commandment of the Lord, to do evil in his sight? Thou hast killed Uriah...and hast taken his wife to be thy wife... And DAVID SAID UNTO NATHAN, I HAVE SINNED AGAINST THE LORD. And Nathan said unto David, The Lord also hath put away thy sin; thou shalt not die.* 2 SAMUEL 12:9, 13

From my experience with handling people, I know that these two types of people are found in everyday life. Decide to be a David who sees and admits faults easily. Remember this: Failure to admit faults is a manifestation of pride and stubbornness. God does not like proud people. The Bible says that he resists the proud!

## David Inquired of the Lord About Everything

> *Therefore DAVID ENQUIRED OF THE LORD, saying, Shall I go and smite these Philistines? And the Lord said unto David, Go and smite the Philistines, and SAVE KEILAH. Then DAVID ENQUIRED OF THE LORD YET AGAIN. And the Lord answered him, and said, Arise, go down to Keilah; for I will deliver the Philistines into thine hand.* 1 SAMUEL 23:2, 4

One of the common phrases in the books of First and Second Samuel, is;:"David inquired of the Lord." The principle of David inquiring of the

Lord for direction is one that is important for all of us today.

David defended the people of Keilah and delivered them from evil. When King Saul heard that David was in the city of the people of Keilah, he decided to attack. Naturally, you would have thought that the people of Keilah would protect David from Saul. But David, as a matter of routine, inquired of the Lord.

> *THEN SAID DAVID, Will the men of Keilah deliver me and my men into the hand of Saul? And the Lord said, They will deliver thee up.* 1 SAMUEL 23:12

To his surprise, the Lord told him that the people whom he had just saved would betray him and hand him over to Saul. David must have been surprised when the Lord told him, "These people will be ungrateful to you. They will hand you over to Saul for your execution."

**David saved his life by this act of inquiring of the Lord.** If David had not had these principles, his life would have been cut short. If he had not developed the habit of waiting on the Lord, he would have died as a young man. David's ministry would have ended years earlier if he had not used this important principle.

There are times that the Lord has shown me things that are contrary to my understanding. The ministry is a supernatural vocation. The fact that you use your mind to make decisions does not mean that you should not listen to the Holy Spirit. I use my mind a lot, but I rely more on the supernatural guidance of the Holy Spirit. Thank God for our minds. But the Holy Spirit is leading us everyday of our lives. "For as many as are led by the Spirit of God, they are the sons of God" (Romans 8:14).

If it were not necessary for God to lead us by His Spirit, He would not waste His time. Listen to the voice of the Holy Spirit and you will walk into success.

## David Was Religious

David was a very religious person. He did not leave spiritual things to the prophets and pastors alone. Although he was a king, his heart was in spiritual matters. You can see the type of person he was from the Psalms he wrote. David spoke of living in the temple of God. He thought of staying in church for long hours.

> *For A DAY IN THY COURTS is better than a thousand. I had rather be a doorkeeper in the house of my God, than to dwell in the tents of wickedness.* PSALM 84:10

> *I WAS GLAD when they said unto me, Let us go into the house of the Lord.* PSALM 122:1

David organized the transfer of the Ark of the Covenant to Jerusalem. It was very important to him that these things were done. I believe that making God a central figure in your life is vital to success. David wanted to build a temple and a church. How many politicians and people of power think about building a church? How many would say that they'd like to stay in church for long periods?

People with wealth and influence often fight against the church. They lift themselves up as proud and arrogant elements capable of destroying the church. Learn a lesson from David. His heart was in the church. His vision was to build God a grand temple. This is what I mean by being religious. No matter your profession, you can make God the center of your activities. God is not blind. He will see and reward you because you love Him.

Psalm 91 tells us that because you have set your love on God, He will remember you in your time of trouble. He will lift you up and establish you. Let Jesus be the center of your life and you will enjoy the blessings of Jehovah.

# CHAPTER 13

# The Art of Following Solomon

## Solomon Started Building the Church Immediately

The most notable event of Solomon's ministry was the building of the temple. Still today, you hear the phrase, "Solomon's temple." Solomon was the one who built a beautiful temple for Jehovah. There was no temple like the one he built. His father David could not build the temple because of the many wars he fought.

### Blessed in His Old Age

**One of the secrets to prolonging your days on this earth is be involved in the building of the house of God. Some years ago, I noticed a man who was really blessed of God.** The man had lived to a ripe old age and had many children and grandchildren. In his old age, he was rich and in good health. Most people at that age would be flat broke! Most of the people I know in that age group depend on their children for survival. But this man did not depend on his children at all. Rather, some of his children depended on him.

I asked the Lord, "Why is this man blessed?" The Lord showed me that this man was a person very much involved in the building of the church. He had spent a lot of his personal money building the church. The Spirit of God whispered to me, **"The people who involve themselves in building the church, whether spiritually or physically have a special grace upon their lives."**

Do you remember the centurion who needed a miracle for his servant? The people told Jesus the man deserved a miracle because he had built them a synagogue.

> *And when they came to Jesus, they besought him instantly, saying, That HE WAS WORTHY for whom he should do this: For he loveth our nation, and HE HATH BUILT US A SYNAGOGUE.* Luke 7:4, 5

They said, "This man is worthy because he built us a synagogue." Good things from Jesus were about to flow into this man's life because he had built a church.

Years ago, I heard a great man of God ministering at the sod-cutting ceremony of a church in my city. This man of God made a statement that I will never forget. He told the congregation, **"Build God's house, and God will build a house for you."** I have never forgotten those words. Build a house of stability and safety for God's people and God will make your dwelling secure.

## Solomon Prayed for Wisdom Rather Than the Fruits of Wisdom

Solomon was having a prayer time and asked the Lord to give him an understanding heart to discern between good and bad.

> *In Gibeon the Lord appeared to Solomon in a dream by night: and God said, Ask what I shall give thee. Give therefore thy servant an understanding heart to judge thy people, that I may discern between good and bad: for who is able to judge this thy so great a people?* 1 Kings 3:5, 9

The Bible teaches us that his prayer pleased God. The Bible tells us that God said, "Because you didn't ask for riches or long life, but have asked for understanding, I'm going to give you wisdom. In addition, I'm going to bless you with fantastic riches which you didn't ask for."

> *Behold, I have done according to thy words: lo, I have given thee a WISE AND AN UNDERSTANDING HEART...*
> *And I have also given thee that which thou hast not asked, both RICHES, AND HONOR...* 1 KINGS 3:12, 13

Solomon had the chance of a lifetime. He asked God for what he wanted. The Lord was impressed by Solomon's desire to seek wisdom in order to be able to rule well. Let's face it, how many of us really seek for righteousness and wisdom from God? The Bible says in Matthew 6:33, **"But Seek ye first the kingdom of God, and his righteousness; and all these things shall be added unto you."**

There are lay people who look at me and say, "Oh, it's okay for you to be in full-time ministry; you come from a rich family. You don't have to lose anything," they say. "Even if you don't work, your father will give you money."

I often smile and say nothing. I realize that these people do not even believe that I genuinely chose between secular riches and God's work. I know in my heart that that was the choice I made. I decided to build God's house instead of my own life. If God has blessed me because of that, I do not apologize for the blessings of God. I give Him the glory.

I challenge you to seek after righteousness as Solomon did. It may not seem to be the most direct route to prosperity and riches, but that is the route that God has set. You cannot be wiser than God. Seek first the kingdom of God and His righteousness!

Decide to live a holy life. Pay the price and live for God. As you take up your cross to follow Him, the angels of heaven will take note. The kingdom of heaven will acknowledge that you are on the right road. You will be rewarded with the things that all men are seeking. They will be added to your life. You will experience prosperity without chasing after it!

## Solomon Used His Mind in Being Spiritual

Did you know that the difference between human beings and most animals is the size of their brains? The size of the brain and the use of the mind is a key difference between human beings and animals. Those who have a mind can think, reason and rule. **Those who use their minds rule over those who don't.** A person who does not use his mind is no different from a person who does not have one!

When God created us, He blessed us with the ability to think and to reason. When you become born-again, it does not mean that you should not use your mind anymore. **A common mistake of spiritual Christians is that they stop using their minds!** I am a spiritual person, but I believe in using my mind. The fact that I am born-again does not mean that I do not think anymore.

When I was in secondary school, most of the Scripture Union leaders did not pass their exams. It was as though as sooon as you became spiritual and prayerful, the mind stopped working. This is a fallacy. There are two types of Christians: those who use their minds and those whose minds are on vacation!

If you are going to cross a major highway, you do not close your eyes and say, "Lord, when I hear Your voice, I will begin to cross the road." That is nonsense! God expects you to use your eyes and mind to make the right decision. If you stop using your mind, you are insulting God.

The reason why we can catch lions and put them in cages is because we have a superior mind. The reason why we can trap poisonous snakes and wild tigers is that our mind gives us the upper hand over these animals.

**Making full use of your intellectual capabilities will give you the upper hand in this life.** It has been proved that all ethnic groups of the human race, have equally sized and equally capable brains. **That means that all human beings are equal in their thinking ability and in intelligence.** That is why there are equally capable white and black heart surgeons. That is why there are equally capable airline pilots and scientists of all nationalities.

But it is a sad fact of history that some races have gained superiority over others. Some nations have even captured and dominated others for years.

Today, in a very civilized world, many nations are economically enslaved to other nations. The world is made up of rich and wealthy nations that rule and dominate the poor and underdeveloped ones.

### The Thinker Controls the Non-Thinker

I have found that when a group of people become too emotional and spiritual, they often do not use their minds fully. People who use their minds fully usually dominate people who don't. **You control a person when you think more than he thinks**. Have you not noticed that men are often more calculating and logical than women? Women are often more emotional than rational. Is it not true that, generally speaking, men rule over women? I believe in prayer. I believe in fasting. I believe in the Holy Spirit and I believe in the supernatural. That does not cause me to shut down my mind.

## Solomon Sought Wisdom, Knowledge and Understanding

Solomon asked for wisdom. He was planning to use his mind! The Bible teaches us that wisdom will promote us. It also tells us that wisdom will cause us to come to an honorable end. The Bible says with all your getting, get wisdom.

> *Wisdom is the principal thing; therefore get wisdom: and with all thy getting get understanding. Exalt her, and she shall promote thee: she shall bring thee to honor, when thou dost embrace her.* PROVERBS 4:7, 8

People, who have used the mind God has given them, are ruling over those who have not used the gift of the mind. Some people use their brain to invent airplanes, cars and ships. Those who invent airplanes are from the rich nations. Those who just buy and use these things are not as wealthy. Those who have made the great inventions are ruling over the rest.

America dominates in many things. There is hardly an invention, from cars to computers to spacecraft, that doesn't come from the western world.

In many countries, the American dollar is used as a financial yardstick for transactions. On the contrary, African currencies are hardly used anywhere else in the world.

## The Lagoon God Says "No!"

Many times, development and progress in underdeveloped countries is stifled for emotional and spiritual reasons. When a lagoon should be developed into a tourist resort, the people oppose it using spiritual reasons.

The lagoon god does not like to be disturbed. The lagoon god says, "No," and therefore there will be no development. When foreign investors come to develop certain portions of land, the ancestors (the dead) do not like it because their resting place is being disturbed and it will invoke curses.

I once visited a beautiful lake in Africa. The people living near this lake used logs, instead of boats, to cross the lake. Apparently, the gods do not like certain types of vessels on the lake! As I watched people paddling on logs, I asked myself whether we were in the Stone Age or in the twentieth century.

I marvelled as I realized how far back human beings could be when the mind is not allowed to function in a logical, sagacious, discerning and rational manner. When we allow spiritual and emotional factors to lead at the expense of common sense, we can only expect a hard life. God gave us the gift of the mind. He also gave us emotions and a soul. You are supposed to use all these components of your being.

As you travel around the world you will realize one thing -- educated people are in-charge everywhere. Education develops the mind. Those who are educated are those who have developed one of God's greatest gifts to man -- the mind.

The human mind is more complicated than any computer. It is a supernatural gift from God. He expects us to think and to reason. God expects us to develop and to use this great gift of the mind! The Bible says that the wise man sees the evil ahead and keeps himself, but the simple passes on and is punished. Simplicity cannot help us in this modern day and age.

I sometimes watch African soccer teams. They carry fetish priests and Juju men to the football fields to ensure that they win the matches. Some goalkeepers place special charms within the goalposts to prevent the ball from entering. During the half-time break, the "Juju" man gives assurances, chants and casts more spells and charms over the players.

Meanwhile, their western and European counterparts are receiving scientifically formulated intravenous infusions in their changing room. They are enhancing their performance by scientific means.

Is it a wonder that those who use these scientific methods have more consistent and favourable results? How many African teams have even participated in the finals of the World Cup? Which African team has ever won the World Cup, in spite of all the fetish and charms invoked?

> *Then said I, WISDOM IS BETTER THAN STRENGTH: nevertheless the poor man's wisdom is despised, and his words are not heard.* ECCLESIASTES 9:16

The Bible teaches that wisdom is better than strength. You may have a lot of brute strength like a lion. However, the one who is using his mind is going to rule over you. The Bible says, "Wisdom is better than strength." When you stop using your mind, you lower yourself. People who are using their minds will rule over you and dominate. **No matter how spiritual you are, your mind is a gift from God and you must use it.**

Culture is a good thing, but when it goes against all forms of progress, we must ask ourselves whether that tradition should not be abolished. A country like Japan is said to have over six million gods. However, it seems to me that the gods of Japan have not opposed the sound and rational development of their country. In fact, I wouldn't be surprised if the gods of Japan encouraged development! I am not against culture and tradition, but I am against poverty, backwardness and the lack of education. I'm sure it's the same with you.

If you want to get married, you have to use your mind. You cannot just say that the Spirit is leading you to marry. Of course, you must follow the leading of the Spirit, but you are expected to use your mind. What is the background of your proposed wife? Do you really know her?

> *Wisdom is the principal thing; therefore get wisdom: and with all thy getting get understanding. Exalt her, and she shall pro-*

> *mote thee: she shall bring thee to honor, when thou dost embrace her.* PROVERBS 4:7, 8

### The Wisdom of God

Some Pentecostal churches are not respected because they are so spiritual that they leave their minds out of important decisions. **The finances of the church are not managed by using anointing oil. They are administered using sound financial and accounting principles.** A pastor may be highly anointed with miracles but when it comes to matters of land, law, property and finances, the mind and education must come into play.

Did you know that Solomon did not have as much military strength as his father David? David was a fighter and was known for winning wars. But look at Solomon. He had more peace than his father did. **How did Solomon establish himself in peace and stability?** He made friends with all his neighbours and had many allies. Solomon had far more peace in his day than David his father. *Wisdom was once again proving to be better than strength.*

> *And Solomon made affinity with Pharoah king of Egypt...*
> 1 KINGS 3:1

> *And the Lord gave Solomon wisdom, as he promised him: and there was peace between Hiram and Solomon; and they two made a league together.* 1 KINGS 5:12

In this passage, Solomon used the wisdom of God in ruling the nation. He developed internal stability by using the wisdom of God. The use of his mind was giving him the upper hand. He was becoming more famous than even his father David.

The name of the church is often dragged through the mud. I believe in deliverance. I believe in the power of healing. I believe in miracles. But I also believe in using the wisdom of God. I believe that pastors must be well educated in order to be sound ministers of the gospel. Wisdom is still the principal thing and we need to use the mind if we are to truly follow Solomon.

Parents, push your children as far as they can go in education. They will one day thank you because you helped them to develop their minds.

I believe very strongly in the power of the Holy Spirit. I believe in the anointing. If you were to visit any of our miracle services, you would see the power of God at work. We have a flow of the Spirit of God and we experience all kinds of manifestations. People fall under the power, people laugh in the Holy Ghost and people cry.

Many people shake and tremble under the anointing and power of the Spirit. Sometimes entire sections of the congregation are slain (?) in the Spirit as the power of God moves like a wave through them. I speak in tongues more than I speak in English. I spend hours waiting on the Lord in prayer and fasting. However, none of these have made me send my mind away on a vacation. God gave me my mind and I intend to use it.

My mind needs to be alert in order for me to make important decisions that concern the administration and smooth running of my ministry. I have heard the Holy Spirit speaking to me in my heart many times. I believe in what He tells me and I obey Him. But my mind is still alert and active. I try to understand and reason out every commandment that the Lord gives me.

Most Christians are either so emotional or spiritual that they have no use of their minds. Others are so logical and rational that the Spirit of God cannot move in their lives and churches. **The key here is to balance the Spirit with wisdom.**

That is the will of God. Every Christian leader must learn to achieve a balance between the power and the wisdom.

> *But unto them which are called, both Jews and Greeks, CHRIST the POWER of God, and the WISDOM of God.*
> 1 CORINTHIANS 1:24

I have highlighted the words: *Christ, Power* and *Wisdom*. That is what I want you to get as you read this book. Christ Jesus is not only power to us. He is *power* and *wisdom*. When you are able to effectively combine the power and the wisdom, you are then truly following Solomon.

## Solomon Remembered His Father's Words

One of Solomon's secrets was to obey his father's instructions. King David, Solomon's father, left him several important instructions as he lay dying on his bed. Solomon obeyed all of them!

> *Children, OBEY YOUR PARENTS in the Lord: for this is right. Honor thy father and mother; which is the first commandment with promise; That it may be well with thee, and thou mayest live long on the earth.* EPHESIANS 6:1-3

If you obey your father, it will be well with you. If you do not obey your father and mother, it will not be well with you - It is as simple as that! Solomon's kingship was established because he took his father's words seriously and obeyed each instruction to the letter. Solomon would never have become what he became if he had ignored his father's instructions.

### Different Types of Fathers

God gives every human being a father and a few father-figures. You have a father after the flesh, which is your biological father. You may also have a father-in-law, your spouse's father or even an adopted father. Your father-in-law can be a blessing to you if he is a good person. Moses was blessed tremendously by his father-in-law, Jethro.

You can have a spiritual father -- someone who brought you to Christ and established you in the Lord. Another important type of father is a father-in-ministry. This is someone who brings you up and helps you to be established in the ministry. All these types of fathers are important to us.

It is important to understand the principle of honoring fathers and mothers. Many church leaders have walked out into a spiritual abyss by violating these simple principles. Some ministers disappear into oblivion by dishonoring the fathers that have been set in the land.

Before King David died, he called his son Solomon to his bedside and gave him some instructions. As Solomon looked upon his dying father, perhaps some thoughts ran through his mind. The man lying on the bed was someone who had made many mistakes in his life. He had committed adultery with Bathsheba and had disgraced the nation. He had murdered one of his own soldiers. David's own children had been involved in the rape and murder of each other.

In his latter days, David had not been able to keep his family together. It was this same ailing father, who was giving instructions to Solomon. Solomon obeyed his father! Because of that obedience, Solomon prospered to the point that silver became like stones to him.

# CHAPTER 14

# The Art of Following Nehemiah

## Nehemiah Was Concerned About the House of God and the People of God

The words of Nehemiah the son of Hachaliah. And it came to pass in the month Chisleu, in the twentieth year, as I was in Shushan the palace, That Hanani, one of my brethren, came, he and *certain* men of Judah; and I ASKED THEM CONCERNING THE JEWS that had escaped, which were left of the captivity, AND CONCERNING JERUSALEM.

And they said unto me, The remnant that are left of the captivity there in the province are in great affliction and reproach: the wall of Jerusalem also is broken down, and the gates thereof are burned with fire.

> *And it came to pass, WHEN I HEARD THESE WORDS, THAT I SAT DOWN AND WEPT, and mourned certain days, and fasted, and prayed before the God of heaven,*
>
> Nehemiah 1:1-4

I once read a book that showed a vision of Jesus during His time on earth. I was sad as I read the discourse in which an angel said that most men were not interested in God.

Are men interested in God? Quite frankly, my experience as a pastor leads me to think that people are not. I find that most people who come to church on Sunday mornings are interested in themselves and in their own prosperity. They want to have good families, good cars, good homes and good futures.

Most people are not concerned about the church and its welfare. They give tithes and offerings when they think or feel it will benefit them somehow. This is sad, and it makes me feel helpless and depressed.

But Nehemiah was different. He was concerned about the church and people of God. He was concerned about Jerusalem and its welfare. He dwelt in the king's palace and had a good job. He was a secure and blessed person needing nothing in that sense. And yet he was concerned about the house of God.

One day, a rich man was questioned about why he was a faithful church attendee. "What do you need?" they asked him.

"Why do you go to church? What problems do you have? What do you pray for and what makes you go to church?"

As far as they were concerned, people only went to church when they had problems.

Listen to me, dear friend. One of the master keys to becoming a successful person is to be concerned about the house of God and its welfare. Be concerned about the church building! Be concerned about the church's finances! Be concerned about the church members! This is the key characteristic that marked out Nehemiah and made him different from all others we read about in the bible.

## Nehemiah Had a Good Attitude

> *And it came to pass in the month Nisan, in the twentieth year of Artaxerxes the king, that wine was before him: and I took up the wine, and gave it unto the king. NOW I HAD NOT BEEN BEFORETIME SAD IN HIS PRESENCE.*
>
> Nehemiah 2:1

When Nehemiah's attitude changed, it was immediately noticed by the king. Nehemiah was someone who constantly had a good attitude at work. His face was bright; he was cheerful and happy at work. A moody, sulky face was not what the king was used to dealing with. The change in the eager and cheerful face of Nehemiah was so noticeable that it sparked off a chain reaction.

No one wants to have an unhappy and unlucky person around him.

Everyone wants to have a cheerful and encouraging person by his side. Most leaders are lonely and discouraged. They constantly sense danger and pretence. What a joy it is to have a positive and happy person around you!

Just as good looks and appearances are important and have a great role to play in a person's success, your positive attitude and countenance will equally work in your favour. A smiling and happy face is something many people would pay to have.

## Nehemiah Built the House of God in Spite of Accusations

> *But when Sanballat the Horonite, and Tobiah the servant, the Ammonite, and Geshem the Arabian, heard it, they laughed us to scorn, and despised us, and said, what is this thing that ye do? WILL YE REBEL AGAINST THE KING?* NEHEMIAH 2:19

Accusation is the reward you must expect for your good works. Accusations are the "thank yous" that are dished out to people who have bent over backwards to help and to love.The accusations against Nehemiah would have stopped a *lesser person* but not Nehemiah.

To be stopped by accusations which are levelled against you is to demonstrate that you are a lesser kind of person. To be stopped by accusations is to reveal that you are not strong enough and that you do not have the resilience and the tenacity it takes to accomplish your calling.

John Wesley was accused of many things throughout his life. He demonstrated that he was made out of something stronger and tougher than those accusations. I always remember a statement somebody made of John

Wesley and I want to share that with you. It was, "A 'lesser person' would have been stopped and driven out of ministry." I always think about that phrase ("a lesser person"). What did he mean by a "lesser person"?

If that statement is true, there are stronger and more tenuous persons in life and there are weaker and lesser persons! A "lesser person" will have less character, less strength, less resolve, less resilience and less determination to fulfil his calling against all odds. A lesser person will consider the difficulties as a sign to quit.

Why not decide that you will be a greater and stronger person! Why be a lesser light when you can be a greater light? The accusations against your person must reveal that you are a greater person.

## Nehemiah Built the House of God in Spite of Fear

*And OUR ADVERSARIES SAID, THEY SHALL NOT KNOW, NEITHER SEE, TILL WE COME IN THE MIDST AMONG THEM, AND SLAY THEM, AND CAUSE THE WORK TO CEASE.*

*And it came to pass, that when the Jews which dwelt by them came, they said unto us ten times, From all places whence ye shall return unto us they will be upon you.*

*Therefore set I in the lower places behind the wall, and on the higher places, I even set the people after their families with their swords, their spears, and their bows.*

*And I looked, and rose up, and said unto the nobles, and to the rulers, and to the rest of the people, BE NOT YE AFRAID OF THEM: REMEMBER THE LORD, which is great and terrible, and fight for your brethren, your sons, and your daughters, your wives, and your houses.* NEHEMIAH 4:11-14

Fear is an enemy you will have to overcome if you want to build the house of the Lord. However, this is a much more difficult enemy to overcome than ridicule. Why is that? There are a lot of genuinely frightening things in this world. Nehemiah faced genuine dangers in his quest to build the walls of Jerusalem. There are many things that can inspire fear in the hardiest of people. There are many things out there that can kill you, destroy you and scramble your life forever. It doesn't take much to see these things.

When God sends you, you will see these dangers and frightening things everywhere. It does not take long for fear to build up in you. I have always been afraid whilst I obeyed the Lord. Obeying the Lord does not take away fear. That is why He says, "Fear not. Only believe." It is the only way to go.

Do you think David was not aware of the danger he faced when he challenged Goliath? He must have been terrified! Indeed, Nehemiah was terrified when he heard what Sanballat and Tobiah were saying. But he still went ahead and built the walls of Jerusalem. He told his followers: "Be not ye afraid of them: remember the Lord, *which is* great and terrible, and fight for your brethren, your sons, and your daughters, your wives, and your houses."

## Nehemiah Worked Night and Day

> *Nevertheless we made our prayer unto our God, and set a watch against them DAY AND NIGHT, because of them.*
> NEHEMIAH 4:9

Most people want to work only in the day. But Nehemiah worked both day and night. Do you have a desire to leave work early, to come in late and to do as little as possible? Analyze yourself and see whether you are constantly looking for a chance to have a day off. How often do you come up with deceptive reasons to skip a day of work? You are obviously someone who is not going to prosper the way Nehemiah prospered.

The key to successfully waging war is to concentrate all your forces on a point until it yields to the pressure that you are applying. This is the principle that Nehemiah used to build the wall of Jerusalem. He worked day and night until the project was done.

Working only during the day or when it is convenient does not help to complete projects. People often ask me, "When do you find time to write books?"

Simply put: You can do something great if you are ready to build day *and* night.

## Nehemiah Was Not Distracted nor Side-tracked

> *And I sent messengers unto them, saying, I am doing a great work, so that I cannot come down: WHY SHOULD THE WORK CEASE, WHILST I LEAVE IT, AND COME DOWN TO YOU?* NEHEMIAH 6:3

Nehemiah refused to leave his work and follow vain things. "Why should I leave my work, and come down to you?" he asked. You will be distracted when you try to impress people. Impressing people is the greatest distraction on your calling and ministry. *People who love to impress on the outside are rarely impressive on the inside.* It takes time and effort to impress people, and this becomes the greatest distraction from the time and effort needed to be impressive on the inside. You will have to cease the good work you are doing on the inside so that you can attend to impressing people on the outside.

Do not be distracted from your original calling. Do not be distracted from the "real" thing. Give your attention to the main thing. The main thing is still the main thing.

Believers who focus on being pleasing and friendly to everyone rarely have time to be pleasing and friendly to God whom they serve. Useless socializing and watching television are key distractions from your principal calling.

## Nehemiah Ignored the Threat of Death

> *Afterward I came unto the house of Shemaiah the son of De-*

> *laiah the son of Mehetabeel, who was shut up; and he said, Let us meet together in the house of God, within the temple, and let us shut the doors of the temple: for they will come to slay thee; yea, in the night will they come to slay thee.*
>
> *AND I SAID, SHOULD SUCH A MAN AS I FLEE? AND WHO IS THERE, THAT, BEING AS I AM, WOULD GO INTO THE TEMPLE TO SAVE HIS LIFE? I WILL NOT GO IN.* NEHEMIAH 6:10-11

There are many things that can take away your life on this earth.That is why birthdays are celebrated with such zeal. I once heard some amazing statistics about the different causes of death. It is said that your chances of dying in an airplane are in the region of 1: 5,000. It also said that your chances of dying out of a car accident are 1:85 and your chances of dying out of cancer is 1:9. Amazingly, the more you know, the more you realise how much of a miracle it is to be alive.

You must fulfil your calling in spite of the threats and risk of death. There is death and dying all around. But it must not guide you and it must not be the reason for the things you do not do.

Although you can die from many different causes you must know and believe that death is a predetermined thing. God predetermines it. The Scripture says that the days of a man are determined by God. "Seeing his days are determined, the number of his months are with thee, thou hast appointed his bounds that he cannot pass" (Job 14:5). "Is there not an appointed time to man upon earth? Are not his days also like the days of an hireling" (Job 7:1)?

Nehemiah was successful because the threats and dangers of death did not guide him. There was a group of people who once set out to sea to discover for themselves what lay beyond the horizon. They discovered the world at the risk and peril of their own lives. They wanted to find out whether the world was flat and whether they would fall off at the end. In deed, they did not fall off but became the conquerors and rulers of the whole world.

There was a group of people who wanted to find out whether there was life on the moon. This group wanted to find out what planets, stars and galaxies exist. They engaged in expeditions and experiments at the expense of their very own lives. This is exactly what Nehemiah did and that is why he achieved great things for God in spite of the risks and dangers to his personal life.

There is another group of people who show little interest in how high a mountain is or what lies behind a mountain. Is there anyone on the other side? Are there any animals to discover? Is there an advanced civilization that may be discovered? These are not questions that occur to this group of people. Safety first! Nehemiah did not operate by this passive and disinterested attitude. He did not live his life by a "safety first" policy. That is why he achieved great things for God.

## Nehemiah Overcame False and Fear-Filled Prophecies

> *And, lo, I perceived that God had not sent him; but that HE PRONOUNCED THIS PROPHECY AGAINST ME: FOR TOBIAH AND SANBALLAT HAD HIRED HIM.*
>
> *THEREFORE WAS HE HIRED, THAT I SHOULD BE AFRAID, and do so, and sin, and that they might have matter for an evil report, that they might reproach me.*
>
> *My God, think thou upon Tobiah and Sanballat according to these their works, and on the prophetess Noadiah, and the rest of the prophets, that would have put me in fear.*
>
> NEHEMIAH 6:12-14

Satan knows that fear is one of the most potent guiding forces. If you can get people to be afraid of something, you can get them to avoid it. If you can get them to be afraid of the mission field, you can stop them from going there. If you can get people to be afraid of the ministry, you can keep them from entering it.

Thank God for the prophetic ministry. How I wish I were more of a prophet! How I pray for visions and dreams! How unfortunate it is that many who are endowed with this gift use it to frighten and control human beings. It is the easiest thing to come forth with a fear-filled prophecy.

There are so many bad things that we fear, and the people of God are so ready to receive a prophecy that will avert any of these bad things. Unfortunately, one of the great sources of the evil spirit of fear is fear-filled manipulative prophecies. These are prophecies that minister to fear of bad events and misfortune. Nehemiah had his fair share of fear-filled prophecies, but he stood his ground and he refused to be influenced by an evil-guiding demon of fear.

Any time I hear of things that inspire fear, I am wary of the presence of an evil-guiding demon. Once you yield yourself to fear, your whole life will be escorted along by this evil-guiding spirit. Not all evil spirits that guide and influence. Some evil spirits torment, others harass and intimidate, whilst yet others accuse and oppress. But the spirit of fear frightens, guides and escorts believers until they are outside the will of God.

Nehemiah did not respond to the fear that was ministered to him. Because of that, he became the famous builder of the walls of Jerusalem.

## Nehemiah Read the Bible

> *And all the people gathered themselves together as one man into the street that was before the water gate; and they spake unto Ezra the scribe to bring the book of the law of Moses, which the Lord had commanded to Israel.*
>
> *And Ezra the priest brought the law before the congregation both of men and women, and all that could hear with understanding, upon the first day of the seventh month.*
>
> NEHEMIAH 8:1-5

The reading of the Word of God is one of the greatest keys to success. Many years ago, I met a lady who introduced me to the greatest key to success: the key of reading the Word of God. In it, you will find all the wisdom and direction you need for your life and ministry.

It is exciting to have visions and dreams. I have heard prophets describe fantastic visions which made them seem so supernatural and out of this world. I felt so ordinary and almost "uncalled" when I listened to their testimonies. However, as time went by, I realised that what they had shared was also available to me through the reading of the Word of God.

Reading the Word of God under the revelatory influence of the Holy Spirit is equivalent to those visions and dreams. If you respect the reading of the Word of God and respect the reality of the presence of the Holy Spirit, you will have even more than what some prophets' experience.

Bible reading is not a spectacular experience, but it is equally supernatural. You must respect it. If you want to be as successful as Nehemiah was, you must learn the art of Bible reading. There is no substitute for reading the Bible. You must read your Bible and you must read it everyday if you are to fulfil God's plan and purpose for your life.

# CHAPTER 15

# The Art of Following Esther

## Esther Learned From Those Ahead of Her

*On the seventh day, when the heart of the king was merry with wine, he commanded Mehuman, Biztha, Harbona, Bigtha, and Abagtha, Zethar, and Carcas, the seven chamberlains that served in the presence of Ahasuerus the king,*

*To bring Vashti the queen before the king with the crown royal, to shew the people and the princes her beauty: for she was fair to look on.*

*But the queen Vashti refused to come at the king's commandment by his chamberlains: therefore was the king very wroth, and his anger burned in him.* ESTHER 1:10-12

### Living Signs in Front of You

Many years ago the Lord showed me that everyone was a replacement of someone else. I am a replacement of someone and you are a replacement of someone. There is always a reason why people are replaced. It is important to understand the reasons why you replaced the person ahead of you.

Esther learned from the mistake of Vashti. She knew she must never make the mistake of defying her king and husband. She knew she must never act proudly or she would be cast down as a withered branch. She had to remember the lesson of Vashti!

All throughout the Bible, God allowed His prophets to be living signs before the people. He would have them act out a drama so that the people would see what would happen. In so doing, God gave them a living sign -- a sign that was clear.

### The Day Isaiah was Naked and Barefoot

> *At the same time spake the Lord by Isaiah the son of Amoz, saying, Go and loose the sackcloth from off thy loins, and put off thy shoe from thy foot. And he did so, walking naked and barefoot.*
>
> *And the Lord said, like as my servant Isaiah hath walked naked and barefoot three years for a sign and wonder upon Egypt and upon Ethiopia;*
>
> *So shall the king of Assyria lead away the Egyptians prisoners, and the Ethiopians captives, young and old, naked and barefoot, even with their buttocks uncovered, to the shame of Egypt.*
>
> ISAIAH 20:2-4

People ahead of you are signs from God to you. They are signs of how you can fall and also how you can rise. Because God has graciously given you living signs and living lessons, you must determine not to fall into the exact same problem that destroyed your predecessor.

Whom has God allowed to stumble right in front of you? It is a message to you of what can happen and how to avoid it. There will definitely be problems and temptations that will come to you that you know little or nothing about. But God has allowed certain things to occur in front of you so that you learn first-hand about what to do and what not to do.

## Esther Prepared Herself

> *Now when the turn of each young lady came to go in to King Ahasuerus, after the end of her twelve months under the regulations for the women--for THE DAYS OF THEIR BEAUTIFICATION were completed as follows: SIX MONTHS with oil of myrrh and SIX MONTHS with spices and the cosmetics for women--* ESTHER 2:12 (NASB)

Preparation is the vital key that generates speed and success. Long and proper preparation is necessary for success in almost every sphere of life. Esther prepared long and hard for the day she would meet the king. She planned over a long period and rehearsed ahead of time, training for the specific task that lay ahead of her. Esther used the five keys of successful preparation to make herself ready for her possible role as a first lady.

**Five Keys to Esther's Preparation**

**1. Plan for a long time.** She planned over a long period of time. She had a long time to decide what to do and what to say to the king. Short-term plans are more likely to fail than long-term plans. "Therefore thus will I do unto thee, O Israel: and because I will do this unto thee, PREPARE TO MEET THY GOD, O Israel" (Amos 4:12).

**2. Foresee problems.** Esther foresaw problems that she would encounter. She knew that she would only have a few minutes with a king who was spoiled for choice. She knew she would have to do something impressive within the short time she was given. The king had seen thousands of beautiful girls and was not easily impressed. Also, there were lingering questions. Why was Vashti thrown out? What problems did first ladies often encounter? What could she do to avoid them? "A prudent man foreseeth the evil, and hideth himself: but the simple pass on, and are punished" (Proverbs 22:3).

**3. Rehearse ahead of time.** Esther rehearsed ahead of time. Preparation is often finalised by having a rehearsal. Doing difficult jobs is made possible by practicing and rehearsing. David had practiced killing giants by killing equally dangerous beasts in the wilderness. His rehearsals made him ready to take on the beast called Goliath. God may be giving you rehearsals for your future ministry. Do not despise the opportunities for training.

**4. Train for specific tasks.** Esther trained for her specific task. Preparation involves detailed training for specific jobs. Once you know what you are going to be doing, you can train specifically for the task. There are many things God will use you to do and will train you by giving you tasks which are similar to your future assignment.

**5. Acquire special knowledge.** Esther was taught with special knowledge. Indeed, you need special knowledge to be a wife. You would have needed even more special knowledge to be the wife of Ahasuerus. Preparation involves training with special knowledge. Special knowledge is required for special tasks. If you do not acquire the special knowledge assigned your special task, you will be unprepared to fulfil your calling.

## Esther Took Here Appearance Seriously

> *Now when the turn of each young lady came to go in to King Ahasuerus, after the end of her twelve months under the regulations for the women--FOR THE DAYS OF THEIR BEAUTIFICATION WERE COMPLETED AS FOLLOWS: six months with oil of myrrh and six months with spices and the cosmetics for women--* ESTHER 2:12 (NASB)

Many spiritual people despise the importance of the physical and outward appearance. But the Scripture teaches us to be ready to give an answer to those who glory in the outward. Indeed, the outward appearance has its place and those who trivialise its importance will pay the price. Esther got into this important position by investing in her outward appearance. She spent months preparing to be the most beautiful woman in Persia.

### The Importance of "Natural" Instructions

Every spiritual quest usually has corresponding natural issues that are important to the success of that spiritual mission. You may have to be successfully married for you to be a successful pastor. Marriage is a completely physical and domestic arrangement with many natural obligations and demands. Without fulfilling these, you may not be successful in your spiritual mission.

Do not despise the instruction of the Lord in natural things. They may be seemingly insignificant but when they are from the Lord they will make the difference for your mission. Although golf is just a game, I find my decision to play golf to be one of the most important natural steps I have ever taken. It has become a true aid to my spiritual quest and mission.

A spiritual person often struggles with instructions from the Lord about natural things. Choosing to ignore God's instructions on natural subjects like sex are often costly to spiritual people who prefer to stick their heads in the ground and pretend as if the natural issues are not there.

## Esther Pleased the Right Person in the Right Way

> *So Esther was taken unto king Ahasuerus into his house royal in the tenth month, which is the month Tebeth, in the seventh year of his reign.*
>
> *And the king loved Esther above all the women, and SHE OBTAINED GRACE AND FAVOUR IN HIS SIGHT MORE THAN ALL THE VIRGINS; so that he set the royal crown upon her head, and made her queen instead of Vashti.*
>
> Esther 2:16-17

Different people require different things to please them. Lions eat meat and are not pleased with grass, leaves and herbs. So are human beings who have different desires and peculiarities. To please a man, you must understand what pleases him. Unfortunately, many women try to please a man with the things that please a woman! Men also try to please women with what pleases a man! Indeed, Esther would have had to find out how to speak to the king in a way that would please him.

**Why Did Esther Please the King?**

I suspect that there were two things that Esther did to please the king. First of all, she must have spoken in a way that impressed him. Your communication and ways of speaking are important if you are to please anyone! Ladies who are very quiet and do not speak much, do not easily get married. They may be beautiful, but no one notices or is impressed by them. Often, no one is attracted to them. Beauty alone is not enough to impress a man. Often, it is how a lady speaks that attracts and impresses him.

Secondly, she would have had to please him sexually. The average man is impressed by good and exciting sex.

- Some marriages have "good" food and "bad" sex!
- Some marriages have "bad" food and "good" sex!
- Some marriages even have "bad" food and "bad" sex. (What a shock!)
- The best marriages have "good" food and "good" sex!

To ignore the importance of exciting, innovative and satisfying sex is to be deceptive and hypocritical! A cursory glance at nature and wildlife reveals such a burning desire and need for the male species to copulate and to breed. This innate and sometimes uncontrollable urge is what Christians battle with in order to confine themselves to one partner. A Christian sexual partner has to provide all the sexual needs that are natural, basic, biological and physiological in nature. Esther was a trained, prepared and highly motivated sexual partner to the king.

**Was Esther an Unmotivated Sexual Partner?**

Unfortunately, many Christians have little or no motivation to be good sexual partners. When ladies are lovers and girlfriends to the man they love, they are highly motivated to perform exciting sexual antics. They will do anything, anytime and anywhere to the delight of their uncommitted boyfriend. Yet, these same girls, when married to Christian men, have little or no motivation to perform the manoeuvres they used to.

As wives, they have little motivation because they have a committed Christian guy who they can take for granted. They have little motivation because they have achieved the social status of being married! They have little motivation because they have children and see no further need for "meaningless" sexual acrobatics.

But you will remember that these same unmotivated wives, who turn up their noses at the mention of sex in church, were once highly motivated, agile, aerobic and sexual gymnasts! They used to enthusiastically twirl around their boyfriends belly and skip around in the bedroom without clothes, smiling, laughing and giggling to the delight of their uncommitted boyfriends.

Today, after becoming the wives of committed Christian brothers, having a child or two and having learned to despise their husbands, they have no energy or enthusiasm for what they consider a mundane, boring, dirty and senseless act of intrusion and discomfort.

They have no more thrills or twirls to offer their boring Christian husbands. After all, this Christian husband will never go away because he has too much to lose if he leaves his wife for another.

I suppose that Esther was a highly motivated sexual partner and the king truly enjoyed his night with her. Do you think that Esther told the king that she wasn't feeling well or that she had a headache? Do you think Esther made a face at the king when he tried to have sex with her? Do you think Esther had a bad attitude towards the king that night? Obviously not! Those bad attitudes are the hallmark of unmotivated Christian wives who no longer care about ministering happiness and excitement privately to their husbands.

## Esther Maximized Her Moment

> *So Esther was taken unto king Ahasuerus into his house royal in the tenth month, which is the month Tebeth, in the seventh year of his reign.*
>
> *And the king loved Esther above all the women, and SHE OBTAINED GRACE AND FAVOUR IN HIS SIGHT MORE THAN ALL THE VIRGINS; so that he set the royal crown upon her head, and made her queen instead of Vashti.*
>
> Esther 2:16-17

Like all the other virgins, Esther was to have one night with the king. In that moment she would have to do things and say things that would impress the king. She had a moment of opportunity, a glimpse into glory and she simply had to maximise that moment.

This is often the way life goes. You have just a moment to say the right things and do the right things. If you do not maximise the "moment" and make the most of your opportunity you will lose everything. Many people complain and say, "If I had more time, I could prove myself." "If I had more time, I would be able to say what I really wanted to say." "If I had more time, I would show everybody who I really am."

Unfortunately, there is no time or opportunity for you to prove yourself. You will be presented with brief moments of opportunity and that is when you have to make your mark. It is because people fail to maximise the moment they are given that they fall and fail in life.

The principle of maximising the moment is seen in examinations when you are given an hour or two to write what you know. How to use that hour properly is what takes you forward or backwards.

Job interviews are also based on this principle -- the principle of maximizing the moment. At an interview, you may have ten minutes to look good and to sound good. You may have many things bottled up in you, but you will be given only a moment to express yourself.

**So How Do You Maximise The "Moment"?**

**1. You must anticipate that you will have a very short time to do whatever you have to do.**

**2. You must be aware of stupid things that you must never do during the "moment."** For instance, I was once advised by some of my seniors in medical school not to answer a question in an oral exam by saying, "I don't know!" That answer seemed to anger the professors.

**3. Learn how to do things quickly and in a "moment."** I have been to many places where people offer to serve us some food and drinks. Sometimes they take so long to come up with what they have, that everyone loses interest. It is not just about serving food and drinks but about serving nice food and drinks at the *moment* it is required.

**4. Be yourself and be as natural as possible during the "moment"**

**you have to be impressive.** Why? You must be yourself because your best performance is your most natural performance! Your worst performance will be your made up and artificial presentation. It is so funny to watch people try to speak with an accent, only to give themselves away after a few sentences. A discerning person will always be able to make out the picture of false pretences.

**5. Prepare for the "moment" like Esther did.** When opportunities present themselves, everyone sees how well you have prepared. Most of the super talented artists practise more than anyone else. A close study of their lives will always lead you to a question: "Are these people really talented or do they just practise a lot?"

**6. Be relaxed.** Tension is the thief of your best performance. When it is time to maximise the moment, you do need be relaxed.

## Esther Stayed Small in Her Own Eyes

Oral Roberts said that he was advised by his mother to stay small in his own eyes. This is the problem with promotion. We become "big" in our own eyes and feel we are no longer in need of inputs from those who once guided us.

It is true that you will grow and cut the umbilical cord, but you will always need to maintain the humility that makes you open to input in your "exalted" position. This was the problem with Saul. He did not stay small in his own eyes and became disconnected from God. The prophet told him:

> *And Samuel said, When thou wast little in thine own sight, wast thou not made the head of the tribes of Israel, and the Lord anointed thee king over Israel?* 1 SAMUEL 15:17

Moses, on the other hand, was not too "big" to receive input from his father-in-law. Even though he had seen angels and Jethro had not, he opened himself up to advice from his father-in-law.

Esther remained small in her own eyes. She had grown up in the house of her uncle and heard him advising her all her life. Amazingly, when she became the queen, Uncle Mordecai still had something to say about what she should do and what she should not do. He told her, "Don't tell anyone where you come from. That is my advice for you in your marriage!" This advice was the key to her survival and success as a queen.

> *Esther did not make known her people or her kindred, for MORDECAI HAD INSTRUCTED her that she should not make them known* Esther 2:10 (NASB)

> *Esther had not yet made known her kindred or her people, even as Mordecai had commanded her, for Esther did what Mordecai told her as she had done when under his care.*
> Esther 2:20 (NASB)

Perhaps your father, mother or pastor has yet to give you the advice that will make or break you in the future. Will you be able to receive the inputs? Will you listen to advice in spite of your success and current status? If you want to follow Esther, you must follow her ability to stay small in her own eyes, listening to her father and her mentor even when she was a queen.

## Esther Did Not Grasp At Power, Privilege and Position

> *Then Mordecai commanded to answer Esther, Think not with thyself that thou shalt escape IN THE KING'S HOUSE, more than all the Jews.* Esther 4:13

Esther was prepared to give up the treasured position of living in the king's house. She was prepared to lose her privileges and her recognition for the sake of her high calling. Position-conscious and privilege-conscious people cannot and do not achieve much! This is because the position is more important to them than the job.

Many years ago, a man called Uncle James said to me, "Some people have 'the post' but they don't have 'the job.' And some have 'the job' but don't have 'the post.'" Uncle James was encouraging me to do the job of ministry and not to be too concerned about whether I had the recognised post or position.

You must focus on the job you are called to do, whether it goes with the position, title or not. Esther was in the king's house. The trappings of the palace and the corridors of power in which she walked, were not able to sway her from her real job of saving God's people in their time of need. Concern yourself with your real calling and not with the trappings of power and position.

## Esther Played Her Special Role When it Was Time

You must understand your prophetic significance and purpose at a particular time.

> *For if thou altogether holdest thy peace at this time, then shall there enlargement and deliverance arise to the Jews from another place; but thou and thy father's house shall be destroyed: and who knoweth whether THOU ART COME TO THE KINGDOM FOR SUCH A TIME AS THIS?* ESTHER 4:14

There is a reason why God raised you up -- to do a specific job for Him. Sometimes people do not realise how important they are in God's overall plan. This is because everybody thinks that being a pastor or evangelist is the only important job that a person could be raised up to do. Because of this, most people do not recognize other strategic and prophetic roles that they are supposed to play.

Dear friend, apart from being a pastor or an evangelist, there are many other things that are of great strategic consequence. The ability to recognise wider and varied roles that you may be called to is key to fulfilling your prophetic vision.

Esther's role was to be planted in the king's palace and to speak to her husband in defence of the Jews. She played her part and will never be forgotten for her role in saving God's people. She was never a pastor, an evangelist or even a singer. She was to play the role of an enchanting, enthusiastic and pleasing wife who would one day use her access and favour to save the people of God.

What is your special role? Is it to help a man of God? Is it to provide food for the house of the Lord? Is it to sing? Is it to give comfort? Is it to be a wife? To be an accountant? To help financially? To be a defender? A forerunner? A holy friend? An advisor to an important person? A listener to a lonely leader's rambling discussions? Is it to be an administrator? Is it to be a son or a daughter? Is it to be an intercessor? Is it to be a teacher? An interpreter? Is it to prevent the presence of evil?

For which strategic purpose have you come into this world? Make sure you fulfil it because fulfilling that special role may do more for the will of God than being the pastor of a large church.

## Esther Was Prepared to Lay Down Her Life

> *Then Esther bade them return Mordecai this answer, go, gather together all the Jews that are present in Shushan, and fast ye for me, and neither eat nor drink three days, night or day: I also and my maidens will fast likewise; and so will I go in unto the king, which is not according to the law: and IF I PERISH, I PERISH.* Esther 4:15-16

In a sense, no one becomes anything great unless he is ready to give up his life for his beliefs. There are two ways to give up your life for something. First of all, you could actually die for what you believe or die while doing what you believe in. Secondly, you could do something dangerous which could potentially cost you your life. Esther did not actually die for her people. But what she did could have cost her her life.

When I came into the ministry I did not give up wealth and riches to serve the Lord. I actually had no wealth or riches to give up. The step I took into ministry was a step in which I lost all *potential* wealth and riches due me through my profession. I think that is the same as giving up the wealth and riches.

Abraham did not actually sacrifice or kill his son Isaac, but God rewarded him as though he had. This is an important key in the dynamics of success. People who are successful have often given up their lives for what they believe.

What do you believe in? What have you given your life up for? Esther is remembered eternally because she gave up her life for her beliefs. True, she did not actually die, but she gave up her life for what she believed.

## Esther Remembered Where She Came From

*Listen to me, you who pursue righteousness, who seek the Lord:*
*Look to THE ROCK FROM WHICH YOU WERE HEWN,*
*And to the quarry from which you were dug.*
Isaiah 51:1 (NASB)

Everyone has origins. God's Word encourages us to remember the rock from which we were taken. Esther remembered who she was and where she came from. Because she remembered, Esther was used to save an entire nation.

Your calling is often connected to who you are and where you come from. People who disconnect, dissociate and do not remember where they come from and often fulfil only a fraction of their real calling.

Do you want to fulfil only a fraction of your calling? Certainly not! You must remember where you came from and how you came to be where you are. There are many Africans who desire to be Americans. They spend their lives trying to speak like Americans and never quite make the mark. It is so easy to see through their unreal accents because the reality keeps breaking out. They never have a great ministry because they do not remember (and do not want to remember) their origins. If ministers remembered their origins, they would have larger fields of harvest to work with and larger congregations to preach to.

Your calling is often related to your origins. Your thick accent will not work amongst people who do not have that accent and God knows that very well.

*Then Esther the queen answered and said, if I have found favour in thy sight, O king, and if it please the king, let my life*

> *be given me at my petition, and my people at my request: for we are sold, I AND MY PEOPLE, to be destroyed, to be slain, and to perish. But if we had been sold for bondmen and bondwomen, I had held my tongue, although the enemy could not countervail the king's damage.* ESTHER 7:3-4

Esther remembered where she came from and God used her to do a mighty and strategic work for which she will never be forgotten. Stop having fantasies about God's work! The formula is simple: start in Jerusalem (where you come from); go to Judea, Samaria and then to the uttermost parts of the world! Never forget this: your hometown will always be connected to your calling!

CHAPTER 16

# The Art of Following Daniel

## Daniel Developed the Ability to Work Closely with Important People

**A. Daniel had the ability to work with the prince of eunuchs.**

*Now God had brought Daniel into favour and tender love with the prince of the eunuchs.* DANIEL 1:9

**B. Daniel had the ability to work with King Nebuchadnezzar who appointed him ruler of the Province of Babylon**

*Then the king made Daniel a great man, and gave him many great gifts, and made him ruler over the whole province of Babylon, and chief of the governors over all the wise men of Babylon.*

*Then Daniel requested of the king, and he set Shadrach, Meshach, and Abednego, over the affairs of the province of Babylon: but Daniel sat in the gate of the king.* DANIEL 2:48-49

***C. Daniel had the ability to work with King Belshazzar when he became third ruler.***

> *Then commanded Belshazzar, and they clothed Daniel with scarlet, and put a chain of gold about his neck, and made a proclamation concerning him, that he should be the third ruler in the kingdom.* DANIEL 5:13-29

**D. Daniel had the ability to work with King Darius as one of the three presidents over the one hundred twenty princes of the kingdom**

It pleased Darius to set over the kingdom a hundred and twenty princes, which should be over the whole kingdom. And over these three presidents, of whom Daniel was first, that the princes might give accounts unto them, and the king should have no damage.

> *Then this Daniel was preferred above the presidents and princes, because an excellent spirit was in him; and the king thought to set him over the whole realm.* DANIEL 6:1-3

There are three keys for relating to kings and other important people. They are:

1. The key of *being truthful* and honest.
2. The key of *being yourself* and being real.
3. The key of *respecting* and honoring kings.

**1. The Key Of Being Truthful and Honest**

Daniel used these three keys to gain favour. Many people do the exact opposite of the three keys above, so they are demoted and thrown out of favour. It is so sad to see people violate these keys over and over again. Instead of being real, honest and speaking the truth, people try to flatter important people. A clever king will see through flattery.

To flatter someone is "to praise the person somewhat dishonestly." To flatter someone is to play upon his or her vanity and susceptibility. A clever king will soon see through it all and, instead of getting promoted you will be done away with as a dishonest and dangerous courtier.

I once had a friend who flattered me constantly, praising me about my ministry and various things I was involved in. After a while, I realised that he was playing on my vanity and my susceptibility. I realised that I had been praised somewhat dishonestly. And what do you do with someone who is somewhat dishonest? Do you keep him near you, or do you move away from him?

Belshazzar was the proud son of Nebuchadnezzar. His father had suffered a serious mental illness as a result of pride. This mental illness, lycanthropy (from the Greek word *lukos*, wolf and *anthropos*, man because the person imagines himself to be a wolf, a bear or some other animal), had not taught Belshazzar to be humble. Instead, he also lifted himself up against the most high God.

Daniel had no difficulty in speaking the truth to the king. Speaking the truth respectfully did not lead to Daniel's destruction. It rather led to his promotion.

**2. The Key Of Being Yourself and Being Real**

The next important step is the key of being yourself. There are so many pretentious people who want to gain the favour of important people. They give themselves away so easily by trying to be what they are not. It is not easy to maintain an act for long. How long do you think Rambo can pretend to have so many guns and be able to overcome hundreds of police officers singlehandedly?

Everything acted is unreal. I have watched as people try to develop unreal foreign accents. Sometimes I feel sorry for their tongues, their lips and their mouths. How painfully difficult it must be to constantly have to speak in an unnatural way. So many ladies pretend to be clean, nice-mannered, polite and soft spoken, whereas in reality, they are ill-natured, stubborn and contentious!

It is not so difficult to see through the lipstick, artificial hair, nails and eyelashes. When they snap at their husbands or children you see the real person peeping through the thick cloud of deception and unrealism.

When the king discovers that he is dealing with the real thing, he is attracted to have more because he knows that it is the real thing.

**3. The Key of Respecting and Honoring Kings.**

The third key for dealing with kings is the key of respect and honor. Proud, stubborn and rude people cannot conceal these traits for long. Soon, the prideful attitude will appear through the covers and an insolent remark will pop out, revealing the serpent beneath.

Kings are lonely people and they long for real friends and good company. But they will rarely give up their honor. When an important person detects presumption, pride or a hidden despising attitude, he will get rid of you. Daniel could have spoken rudely to the king because he was doomed. But he spoke respectfully and gave the king his due honor.

Indeed, these three keys above are the simple but profound principles for dealing with important people who can determine your future.

## Daniel Took Other People's Dream Seriously

You will be deceived if you think that the book of Daniel contains only the visions and dreams of Daniel. Actually, half of the book of Daniel is about the dreams of other people.

Other people's dreams can have a profound effect on your life. Your respect for other people's dreams shows your respect for the Holy Spirit and your respect for the gift of God. Respecting other people's dreams also shows your humility. You are humbled because you accept that you are destitute of dreams and visions and are forced to depend on God speaking through someone else.

Amazingly, great prophecies came through the dreams of these unbelieving kings. God spoke into the future through them. Daniel took them seriously and interpreted them. Through this interpretation, he recognized the power of God to speak in any way that He chose to. He recognized the power of God to use anyone that He wanted to. Notice these famous dreams and the effect they had on the ministry of Daniel.

### King Nebuchadnezzar's Dream of the Great Image

*Thou, O king, sawest, and behold a great image. This great image, whose brightness was excellent, stood before thee; and the form thereof was terrible.* DANIEL 2:31

**King Nebuchadnezzar's Dream of the Great Tree**

*Thus were the visions of mine head in my bed; I saw, and behold a tree in the midst of the earth, and the height thereof was great.* DANIEL 4:10

## Daniel Developed Good Prayer Habits

*Now when Daniel knew that the writing was signed, he went into his house; and his windows being open in his chamber toward Jerusalem, HE KNEELED UPON HIS KNEES THREE TIMES A DAY, AND PRAYED, and gave thanks before his God, AS HE DID AFORETIME.* DANIEL 6:10

Daniel prayed a lot. His prayer life and habits are recorded in the Bible. He gave thanks to God and prayed three times every day. We are not capable of doing much good unless the Lord helps us. It is our prayers that open us up to the help of the Lord. Through prayer we can receive the Holy Spirit and the necessary help we need for our lives.

It is usually difficult to do the right things. The right things are often hard and difficult while the wrong things are nice and easy. One of the ways to help yourself do hard and difficult things is to turn them into habits. This is why we teach our children to have certain habits -- so that they will do the difficult things routinely for the rest of their lives.

Daniel had made prayer a habit. This was the best habit he could have developed for himself. By habitualizing prayer, he walked in a level of anointing that few ever do. Being prayerful is something that you must continuously be. You cannot be filled with the Spirit today and assume that you will be filled tomorrow. You must be filled continuously with the Spirit.

Many people are filled with the Spirit but fail to continue to be filled. In times of crisis and great need, they come to God with intense prayers.

God's intention is for you to be filled with the Spirit by praying all the time.

## Daniel Kept His Faith

> *Now when Daniel knew that the writing was signed, he went into his house; and his windows being open in his chamber toward Jerusalem, he kneeled upon his knees three times a day, and prayed, and gave thanks before his God, as he did aforetime.*
>
> *Then these men assembled, and found Daniel praying and making supplication before his God.* DANIEL 6:10-11

Daniel believed in prayer. Being a Prime Minister or being a hated and persecuted Jew would not change his belief in God and in prayer. He kept his faith and carried on with his prayer. It is this commitment to his faith that gave us the famous story of Daniel in the Lion's Den. Daniel's victory in the lion's den is a victory of keeping the faith!

**Which is the Greatest Declaration?**

The apostle Paul ended his ministry with three powerful declarations (2 Timothy 4:7): *"I have finished my course, I have run my race and I have kept the faith."* Of these three, the least powerful statement seems to be, *"I have kept the faith."* But perhaps it is the greatest of the three declarations. To keep the faith is to keep the beliefs that you have always had!

To continue to believe in what you believed at the beginning of your Christian life is indeed an achievement. Many pastors believe in healing when they first hear about it. But as they go along, they lose their belief in miraculous healing. Most pastors have had the experience of praying for people who died shortly after their prayer.

I have had such experiences. Most of us have experienced tragedies that shatter the confidence we had at the beginning of our Christian experience. Indeed, it is a challenge to carry on and still believe in miracle healing, divine provision and divine protection.

Jacob said he had lived for a hundred and thirty years and experienced lots of trouble. "And Jacob said unto Pharaoh, The days of the years of my pilgrimage are an hundred and thirty years: few and evil have the days of the years of my life been, and have not attained unto the days of the years of the life of my fathers in the days of their pilgrimage" (Genesis 47:9).

After a hundred years of trouble it is easy to lose your faith. You can easily say that there is no God, no Jehovah and no Provider. Daniel kept his faith in God and in prayer in spite of the persecution and harassment he experienced.

## Daniel Didn't Let His Handicap (Being a Eunuch) Limit His Ministry

*And the king spake unto Ashpenaz the master of his eunuchs, that he should bring certain of the children of Israel, and of the king's seed, and of the princes; ...*

*Now among these were of the children of Judah, Daniel, Hananiah, Mishael, and Azariah:* DANIEL 1:3-6

Most of us have some kind of a handicap in our lives. Having some kind of problem, financial or social, should not keep you from fulfilling your calling. You have to fix your eyes on eternity and focus on heaven.

Daniel was a eunuch. That means that he had no testicles and therefore no sexual desires. He also had no drive to get married and would not have a wife or children. This indeed was a great handicap for a young man whose life lay ahead of him. In spite of this, Daniel prayed, fasted and ministered in the office of a prophet.

Most people have a thousand reasons why they do not fulfil their ministry.

- Do not allow your lack of education to keep you from obeying the call.
- Do not allow your late start to prevent you from obeying God.
- Do not allow your being a woman keep you from your calling.
- Do not allow your divorce to keep you from ministering the Word of God.

- Do not allow your past wayward life to keep you from becoming a preacher.

*Be like Daniel and minister the word of God in spite of your obvious handicap!* The success of Daniel was dependent on his ability to minister in spite of his glaring handicap – the absence of balls!

## Daniel Took His Visions and Dreams Seriously

> *In the first year of Belshazzar king of Babylon Daniel had a dream and visions of his head upon his bed: THEN HE WROTE THE DREAM, and told the sum of the matters.*
>
> *Daniel spake and said, I saw in my vision by night, and, behold, the four winds of the heaven strove upon the great sea.*
>
> *And four great beasts came up from the sea, diverse one from another.*
>
> *The first was like a lion, and had eagle's wings: I beheld till the wings thereof were plucked, and it was lifted up from the earth, and made stand upon the feet as a man, and a man's heart was given to it.* DANIEL 7:1-2

The key to cooperating with the anointing is to accept, believe in and flow with visions and dreams that God gives to you. Unfortunately, most people do not value dreams that they are given and so they never walk in the anointing for visions and dreams.

Daniel believed in dreams and visions and this made him one of the greatest prophets. You must believe that God can and will speak to you through dreams and visions. Dreams played an important role in the ministry of Jesus. His entrance into the world was guided by a series of dreams to Joseph. The apostle Paul had several visions that guided him. He had clear revelations of the Lord Jesus Christ and was caught up into the third heavens. Indeed visions and dreams, no matter how unclear they are, are important gifts from the Lord.

If you had a dream in which you saw animals, the likes of which are not found on earth, you would probably say that you had eaten too much! Who has heard of a lion or a leopard that has wings? Yet Daniel wrote down the dream because he respected it. He did not despise the Holy Spirit as we often do. When you write down something, it shows how seriously you are taking it. That is why we ask people to write notes when they are in church.

## Daniel Grew in Humility by Recognizing His Ever-Recent Sinfulness

### Daniel's Humble Prayer

> *And I prayed unto the LORD my God, and made my confession, and said, O Lord, the great and dreadful God, keeping the covenant and mercy to them that love him, and to them that keep his commandments;*
>
> *We have sinned, and have committed iniquity, and have done wickedly, and have rebelled, even by departing from thy precepts and from thy judgments:*
>
> *Neither have we hearkened unto thy servants the prophets, which spake in thy name to our kings, our princes, and our fathers, and to all the people of the land.* DANIEL 9:4-6

Daniel's prayer is one of the few recorded detailed prayers of the Bible. It reveals the heart of a humble man who knew his real condition. Most of us do not know our real and pathetic state of sinfulness. Our ministries, our successes, and our human dignity work together to mask our low spiritual state. We are nothing, but we feel important, dignified and even superior to others.

We all speak confidently about sins we feel distant from. But we are silent about the sins that are pressing on us. We sound so righteous when we speak about things that we feel we are not guilty of. In reality, we are guilty of many of the things for which we rebuke others. Indeed, the more spiritual you become, the more you realize your true state of sinfulness.

All throughout the Bible, spiritual revelation has often shown man's pitiful, sinful spiritual condition. Great prophets had to fall on their knees and beg for mercy when their state was revealed.

This consciousness of being a sinful person happened to Isaiah, "Then said I, woe is me! For I am undone; because I am a man of unclean lips, and I dwell in the midst of a people of unclean lips: for mine eyes have seen the King, the Lord of hosts" (Isaiah 6:5).

This reality of being a sinful person also affected Joshua the High Priest. "And he shewed me Joshua the high priest standing before the angel of the Lord, and Satan standing at his right hand to resist him. And the Lord said unto Satan, the Lord rebuke thee, O Satan; even the Lord that hath chosen Jerusalem rebuke thee: is not this a brand plucked out of the fire? Now Joshua was clothed with filthy garments, and stood before the angel. And he answered and spake unto those that stood before him, saying, Take away the filthy garments from him. And unto him he said, Behold, I have caused thine iniquity to pass from thee, and I will clothe thee with change of raiment" (Zechariah 3:1-4).

This reality also dawned on Peter in the boat. "When Simon Peter saw it, he fell down at Jesus' knees, saying, depart from me; for I am a sinful man, O Lord" (Luke 5:8).

You will notice in Daniel's prayer that he considered himself to have equally committed the sins and iniquities he was praying about. The art of following Daniel is the art of becoming more humble about your state of sinfulness.

## Daniel Became God's Beloved

> *Yea, whiles I was speaking in prayer, even the man Gabriel, whom I had seen in the vision at the beginning, being caused to fly swiftly, touched me about the time of the evening oblation.*
>
> *And he informed me, and talked with me, and said, O Daniel, I am now come forth to give thee skill and understanding.*

> *At the beginning of thy supplications the commandment came forth, and I am come to shew thee; for THOU ART GREATLY BELOVED: therefore understand the matter, and consider the vision.* DANIEL 9:21-23

Only two people in the Bible were called "the beloved." "John the beloved" and "Daniel the beloved." John called himself "the disciple whom Jesus loved" and the angel called Daniel "the beloved." There are great similarities between the ministry of John and Daniel. Both of them had fantastic revelations of the end time. Both of them had fantastic revelations of angels and the spirit world.

These visions and dreams are the gifts given to the beloved ones. I wonder what they did to become "the beloved." I guess it was also their great love for God that yielded such closeness to God.

## Daniel Utilized "No Pleasant Bread" Fasting

> *In those days I Daniel was mourning three full weeks. I ATE NO PLEASANT BREAD, neither came flesh nor wine in my mouth, neither did I anoint myself at all, till three whole weeks were fulfilled.* DANIEL 10:1-3

Fasting is an important spiritual exercise for all Christians. It is important to fast because fasting helps to subdue the flesh so that your spirit can dominate your life. To be carnally minded is to be dominated by the flesh! To be spiritually minded is to be dominated by the spirit! "For to be carnally minded is death; but to be spiritually minded is life and peace" (Romans 8:6).

Many Christians have a season when they fast and after that they do not fast. Does this mean that they will be spiritual for only as long as they do not eat? The answer is No. Can we live on this earth without eating? Again, the answer is No. Can we live successfully on this earth without being spiritual? No.

We need to be spiritual and we need to eat. How can we combine the two? The answer is "*no pleasant bread fasting.*" This is a secret that Daniel deployed to maintain his spirituality. To fast by eating no pleasant bread is to *stay spiritual* by changing what you eat, and eating what is not really pleasant to you. "No pleasant bread fasting" also involves *reducing the amount* that is truly pleasant to you.

All-out fasting (fasting without eating at all) is possible for only brief periods of your life. As you grow up, you will be unable to maintain prolonged seasons of absolute fasting. You will need to know how to do the "no pleasant bread fasting." This will be your key to staying spiritual for longer periods. What is the use of becoming super spiritual for three weeks of the year and being carnal for forty-nine weeks of the year?

The "no pleasant bread" fast does not seem as powerful but it becomes more effective and leads to more spirituality. This was Daniel's key. If you practice fasting with "no pleasant bread" you will fast more and you will be able to continue fasting as you get older and physically weaker.

Comparing "all-out fasting" to "no pleasant bread" fasting is like comparing tennis to golf. Tennis leaves you feeling very exercised and very fulfilled. Golf may not seem to provide much of a workout. Indeed, the exercise of walking and playing golf is less strenuous but is effective as an exercise and can continue into your old age. Over all, golf has a much greater benefit to the individual than tennis. Similarly, the overall effect of "no pleasant bread fasting" is long-lived and much more effective.

# PART III

# Following Begins at Home

This book's title calls following an art. It could also have read *The Skills* or *Craft of Following* for indeed, what we have been discussing are key principles and methods for following after God as disciples of Jesus Christ. But calling following an "art" suggests that it is more than just a skill or craft. It also speaks to the distinctive individuality we each have as we follow God. Remember what Psalm 139:13-14 reveals:

"For you created my inmost being;
you knit me together in my mother's womb.
I praise you because I am fearfully and wonderfully made,
your works are wonderful,
I know that full well."

At the moment of conception, God intentionally shaped your individuality with a distinctiveness that extends throughout your life and this also shapes your relationship with the Father. The similarities of how you or I follow Him will be many, but so will be the distinctives. This requires that as we evaluate, support, instruct and exhort one another to love and do good deeds in the Christian walk we also honor God's grace as it covers our following differences and even failures. No two of us will follow in exactly the same way, and this is by God's design.

I believe it is much like the experience of birthing and raising children and growing up in a family. Several children may have the same father and mother, but each child from that union is oh so unique. The atmosphere, the mores, the environment in the family home may be virtually the same, but each child raised and nurtured there develops in his or her own unique way. And, as the children mature, their distinctives widely outpaces their similarities.

So, to conclude this study on The Art of Following, I want to focus on the dynamics of following as found in the relationship between fathers (both spiritual and natural) and their sons and daughters (both spiritual and natural). Fathers, by God's design, cast long shadows in the lives of their children. So too do spiritual fathers and leaders in the lives of their spiritual children and followers. It is critical that we recognize, understand and cooperate with these relational dynamics in the ways God intended so that we may be faithful and obedient followers and enjoy life-long blessings as his reward.

# CHAPTER 17

# Like Father, Like Son

A study of the lives of different sons and their fathers reveals an uncanny pattern of repetition. Sons fall into the exact same problems their their fathers had. History teaches us that people do not learn from history!

Unfortunately, many sons miss the lessons their fathers learned (or should have learned). Some sons dismiss their father's problems as being peculiar only to them. Other sons do not pay attention to the lessons their father provides and fail to heed the advice. The result of these flippant attitudes is that the sons repeat the calamities and catastrophes of their fathers. This pattern is amply displayed in the Bible.

Abraham disowned his wife. He told King Abimelech of Gerar that she was his sister and thereby disowned her. Many years later, his son Isaac did exactly the same thing.

King David had big problems in his life and ministry because he slept with somebody else's wife. His sons ruined their lives by doing exactly the same thing. Amnon may have been angry with his father David for having an affair with Bathsheba, but he ended up raping his own sister Tamar.

Absalom may have been angry with his father David for sleeping with Bathsheba. He may also have been angry with him for not punishing Amnon for the rape of Tamar. David's failure in these areas may have ignited the rebellion in Absalom. But in the end, Absalom himself ended up sleeping with all his father's wives.

Solomon also had his life destroyed by his interaction with women. As wise as Solomon was, you would think he would have learned from his father's mistakes. Perhaps he did. Perhaps he decided that he would marry any woman he felt attracted to. In the end, he married over a thousand women. Solomon's problems with women became even more complicated because they led him away from Jehovah. It is sad to say that Solomon ended up an idol worshipper.

## Seven Reasons Why Problems Can Pass from Fathers to Sons

Pay attention to your father's experiences. Be careful how you criticize your daddy because the devil that fought your daddy will one day fight you. Like it or not, one day, you will have to fight "your daddy's devils." They are just waiting for you to grow up.

One man of God said to me, "People want to retire me! They want me to be removed from my position in this nation. They think I have too many problems." Then he said something I will not easily forget: "When I am gone, the 'thing' that was fighting me will begin to fight them."

This is an eternal principle and you will be wise to grasp it quickly and early. Being critical of a person opens you up to that person's problems for a number of reasons. Many sons have had to swallow their words as they walked in their father's footsteps and made the exact same mistakes.

### 1. Sons murmur and criticize.

Evil spirits operate in the darkness of sin. Murmuring and criticizing are sins and sin opens the door to evil spirits. Sons who criticize their father pay heavily for it. Notice these biblical examples:

The evil spirit of incurable sickness attached itself to Miriam when she criticized Moses.

The evil spirit of death and destruction fell upon the Israelites when they murmured against Moses. None of them passed into the Promised Land.

Similarly, the spirit of demotion, affliction, inferiority and mediocrity came upon Ham when he despised his father. Noah was disgraced and embarrassed by the exposure of his nakedness. But then, Ham and his descendants were disgraced and embarrassed by the mediocrity of their lives.

> *And MIRIAM AND AARON SPAKE AGAINST MOSES because of the Ethiopian woman whom he had married: for he had married an Ethiopian woman.*
>
> *And they said, Hath the LORD indeed spoken only by Moses? hath he not spoken also by us? And the LORD heard it.*
>
> *(Now the man Moses was very meek, above all the men which were upon the face of the earth.)*
>
> *And the LORD spake suddenly unto Moses, and unto Aaron, and unto Miriam, Come out ye three unto the tabernacle of the congregation. And they three came out.*
>
> *And the LORD came down in the pillar of the cloud, and stood in the door of the tabernacle, and called Aaron and Miriam: and they both came forth.*
>
> *And he said, Hear now my words: If there be a prophet among you, I the LORD will make myself known unto him in a vision, and will speak unto him in a dream.*
>
> *My servant Moses is not so, who is faithful in all mine house.*
>
> *With him will I speak mouth to mouth, even apparently, and not in dark speeches; and the similitude of the LORD shall he behold: wherefore then were ye not afraid to speak against my servant Moses?*
>
> *And the anger of the LORD was kindled against them; and he departed.*
>
> *And the cloud departed from off the tabernacle; and, behold, MIRIAM BECAME LEPROUS, WHITE AS SNOW: and Aaron looked upon Miriam, and, behold, she was leprous.*
>
> NUMBERS 12:1-10

**2. Sons mock their fathers and bring a curse upon themselves.**

There are sons who mock their fathers. Even a despising attitude will attract a well-known biblical curse. A son can inherit curses that will give rise to experiencing his father's problems and more.

> *The eye that mocketh at his father, and despiseth to obey his mother, the ravens of the valley shall pick it out, and the young eagles shall eat it.* PROVERBS 30:17

**3. Problems pass to the sons who despise the advice of their fathers. The son becomes a fool.**

There are sons who despise the advice of their fathers. This makes them fools. Being a fool brings many painful hurts in this life. Read it for yourself: "A fool despiseth his father's instruction: but he that regardeth reproof is prudent" (Proverbs 15:5). "… a foolish man despiseth his mother" (Proverbs 15:20).

Becoming a fool creates problems in your life. Had you not despised your father you would not have received those problems. Many sad difficulties in your life are the result of despising your father and mother. You will also notice that many of these problems match those of your father.

> *A fool's lips enter into contention, and HIS MOUTH CALLETH FOR STROKES.* PROVERBS 18:6

**4. Problems pass from fathers to sons because of the son's pride.**

Only when you think you are as good as someone else do you feel free to criticize that person. A humble person does not speak with swelling words of pride. When sons argue with their fathers, they reveal how big and proud they have become. Only pride stirs up contention (Proverbs 13:10). Pride comes before a fall.

The fall of the sons was preceded by their pride. A father's mistakes can unmask a critical spirit in proud children. They speak heatedly and angrily about the person who brought them into existence and made them who they are. They criticize what they do not understand and this spirit of pride opens the door to their own destruction.

> *Pride goeth before destruction, and an haughty spirit before a fall.* PROVERBS 16:18

**5. Problems pass to sons because of their blindness.**

When you are blind you cannot see any good thing in your father. Blindness is the affliction that strikes critical people. There are sons who are blinded because they despise and dishonor their fathers. The blindness is a result of their lack of respect. And this blindness arises when children casually dismiss the importance of their fathers. They are unable to perceive the father's wisdom; they are unable to learn from his experiences, and they are unable to understand why he made the mistakes he did. They do not see or understand his trials and difficulties. And this failure sets them up to walk in exactly the same path.

> *The eye that mocketh at his father, and despiseth to obey his mother, the ravens of the valley shall pick it out, and the young eagles shall eat it.* PROVERBS 30:17

**6. Problems arise because sons do not take their fathers' words seriously.**

Despising your father will cause you not to take what he says seriously. The Bible describes this as 'not holding fast to his words in your life.' Many sons do not pay attention to the details when their fathers try to teach them something. When he explains why certain problems exist, they don't listen. Notice how Solomon urged his son to pay attention to the things he was saying.

> *When I was a son to my father, Tender and the only son in the sight of my mother,*
>
> *Then he taught me and said to me, "LET YOUR HEART HOLD FAST MY WORDS; Keep my commandments and live;*

*Acquire wisdom! Acquire understanding! Do not forget, nor turn away from the words of my mouth.*

*"Do not forsake her, and she will guard you; Love her, and she will watch over you.*

*"The beginning of wisdom is: Acquire wisdom; And with all your acquiring, get understanding.*

*"Prize her, and she will exalt you; She will honor you if you embrace her.*

*"She will place on your head a garland of grace; She will present you with a crown of beauty."*

*Hear, my son, and accept my sayings, And the years of your life will be many.* PROVERBS 4:3-10 (NASB)

**7. A father's problems pass to the son who does not recognize and honor the great men given to him as fathers.**

Desolation is predicted for those who do not recognize the greatness of the people sent to them. Instead of honoring these great men, they kill them. This is exactly what happened to Jesus.

*O Jerusalem, Jerusalem, which killest the prophets, and stonest them that sent unto thee; how often would I have gathered thy children together, as a hen doth gather her brood under her wings, and ye would not!*

*Behold, YOUR HOUSE IS LEFT UNTO YOU DESOLATE: and verily I say unto you, Ye shall not see me, until the time come when ye shall say, Blessed is he that cometh in the name of the Lord." Luke 13:34-35*

## Four Types of Sons

The nature of a son is revealed by his response to his father. Often, the good, the bad and the ugly come out as sons relate to fathers. The Scriptures speak about four types of sons – the prodigal son, the elder son, the beloved son, and the stubborn and rebellious son.

## 1. Characteristics of a Prodigal Son

*And he said, A certain man had two sons:*

*And the younger of them said to his father, Father, give me the portion of goods that falleth to me. And he divided unto them his living.*

*And not many days after the younger son gathered all together, and took his journey into a far country, and there wasted his substance with riotous living.* LUKE 15:11-24

A. A prodigal son goes away from his father and his father's house
B. A prodigal son wants to be as far away from home as possible
C. A prodigal son wastes his life's opportunities
D. A prodigal son recognizes his mistakes in the midst of his life and returns to his father.
E. A prodigal son suffers the loss of many things because of his foolishness and rebellious ways.

## 2. Characteristics of an Elder Son

*Now his elder son was in the field: and as he came and drew nigh to the house, he heard music and dancing.*

*And he called one of the servants, and asked what these things meant.*

*And he said unto him, Thy brother is come; and thy father hath killed the fatted calf, because he hath received him safe and sound.*

*And he was angry, and would not go in: therefore came his father out, and intreated him.*

*And he answering said to his father, Lo, these many years do I serve thee, neither transgressed I at any time thy commandment:*

*and yet thou never gavest me a kid, that I might make merry with my friends:*

*But as soon as this thy son was come, which hath devoured thy living with harlots, thou hast killed for him the fatted calf.*

*And he said unto him, Son, thou art ever with me, and all that I have is thine.*

*It was meet that we should make merry, and be glad: for this thy brother was dead, and is alive again; and was lost, and is found."* LUKE 15:25-32

An elder son:

A. Stays at home with the father.
B. Never commits any major sins.
C. Never strays off the straight and narrow path set for him by his parents.
D. Does not live a life of pleasure and waste.
E. Can develop a self-righteous and judgmental attitude toward people who stray away. Since he has never committed any of these sins himself, he simply cannot understand why people should indulge in such foolishness. Pray that the father will be alive when the prodigal son finally returns. If the prodigal son is left to the mercy of the elder brother it will not turn out well for him.

### 3. Characteristics of a Beloved Son

*And Jesus, when he was baptized, went up straightway out of the water: and, lo, the heavens were opened unto him, and he saw the Spirit of God descending like a dove, and lighting upon him:*

*And lo a voice from heaven, saying, THIS IS MY BELOVED SON, in whom I am well pleased.* MATTHEW 3:13-17

*And after six days Jesus taketh Peter, James, and John his brother, and bringeth them up into an high mountain apart,*

*And was transfigured before them: and his face did shine as the sun, and his raiment was white as the light.*

*And, behold, there appeared unto them Moses and Elias talking with him.*

*Then answered Peter, and said unto Jesus, Lord, it is good for us to be here: if thou wilt, let us make here three tabernacles; one for thee, and one for Moses, and one for Elias.*

*While he yet spake, behold, a bright cloud overshadowed them: and behold a voice out of the cloud, which said, THIS IS MY BELOVED SON, in whom I am well pleased; hear ye him."*
MATTHEW 17:1-5, KJV

On two different occasions, the Heavenly Father called Jesus Christ a beloved Son -- at the beginning of His ministry (the baptism), and at the end of the ministry (the transfiguration). Jesus Christ was called the beloved Son before He had preached a single message or healed one sick person.

A. A beloved son is someone who submits to authority. Jesus was called a beloved son at the very beginning of His ministry when He accepted the humble conditions of His call.

B. A beloved son is a humble son. Jesus was a beloved Son because He submitted to John the Baptist even though He was the Son of God.

C. A beloved son is someone who is obedient to all instructions. A beloved son will obey an instruction whether it makes sense or not and. whether it is easy or difficult. Jesus Christ was not just obedient to nice and easy instructions. He was obedient at every level. Beloved sons are obedient at all the different levels of obedience.

   Indeed, there are different levels of obedience, but a beloved son will distinguish himself at every level. Each level of obedience leads to a different kind of blessing. Jesus Christ obeyed His father in coming to this earth to live amongst men and showing us God's love. Jesus Christ did the ultimate and obeyed His father even unto the death on the cross. Most Christians would struggle with instructions that would lead to their certain death, but not Jesus Christ! He was the quintessential "beloved Son."

### 4. Characteristics of a stubborn and rebellious son

*If a man have a stubborn and rebellious son, which will not obey the voice of his father, or the voice of his mother, and that, when they have chastened him, will not hearken unto them:*

*Then shall his father and his mother lay hold on him, and bring him out unto the elders of his city, and unto the gate of his place;*

*And they shall say unto the elders of his city, This our son is stubborn and rebellious, he will not obey our voice; he is a glutton, and a drunkard.*

*And all the men of his city shall stone him with stones, that he die: so shalt thou put evil away from among you; and all Israel shall hear, and fear.* DEUTERONOMY 21:18-21

*Now you, son of man, listen to what I am speaking to you; do not be rebellious like that rebellious house. Open your mouth and eat what I am giving you.* EZEKIEL 2:8 (NASB)

Stubborn and rebellious sons:

A. Are resistant to instructions.
B. Are opposed to instructions.
C. Dislike the person of their fathers.
D. Dislike the methods of the father.
E. Grow to dislike the ways of the father.
F. Want a different profession from their father's.
G. Want a different lifestyle from their father's.
H. Want to dress, act and do everything differently from their father.
I. Are angry at correction and need to be corrected for being angry at the correction.

## When Sons Are Short-sighted

The prodigal son was obviously short-sighted in his understanding of who his father was. To avoid this mistake yourself, it is critical to recognize these characteristics of short-sighted sons.

## The Short-sighted Son Sees the Relationship with His Father as a Time-related Contract

A short-sighted son sees his relationship with his father essentially as a short-term encounter that he must live through – rather like a lecturer to be endured during a three-year course in the university. This view is in sharp contrast to the permanent and continuous relationship sons are supposed to have with their fathers.

### A Father is a Tree

A long time ago, there was a large mango tree. A little boy loved to come and play around it every day. He loved to climb the tree to the top, eat the mangoes, and take a nap under the tree's shadow. He loved the tree and the tree loved to play with him.

Time went by and the little boy grew up. He no longer played around the tree everyday, but one day the boy came back. The sad looking tree said, "Come play with me." "I am no longer a kid. I don't play around trees anymore," the boy replied." "I want toys. I need money to buy them."

"Sorry, I don't have money, but you can pick my mangoes and sell them. Then you will have money." The boy was so excited. He grabbed all the mangoes on the tree and left happy. But the boy did not come back after he picked the mangoes and the tree was lonely and sad.

One day the boy returned again and the tree was so excited. "Come and play with me," the tree said. "I don't have time to play. I have to work for my family. We need a house for shelter. Can you help me?" "Sorry, but I don't have a house. But you can chop off my branches to build your house." So the boy cut all the branches off the tree and left happy. The tree was glad to see him happy, but the boy did not come back to visit the tree.

The tree was lonely and sad. Then one hot summer day, the boy returned and the tree was so delighted. "Come and play with me," the tree said. But the boy replied, "I am so sad and I am getting old. I want to go sailing to relax myself. Can you give me a boat?" The kind old tree said, "You can use my trunk to build your boat. You can sail far away and be happy." So the boy cut down the tree trunk to make a boat. He went sailing and did not show up again for a long time.

After many years the boy returned again to the same tree. "Sorry, my boy, but I don't have anything for you anymore. No more mangoes for you..." the tree said. "I don't have teeth to bite anyway," the boy replied. The tree said, "I have no more trunk for you to climb on and play." "I am too old for that now," the boy said.

Then the tree said, "I really can't give you anything. The only thing left are my dying roots," the tree said with tears. The boy replied, "I don't need much now, just a place to rest. I am tired after all these years." The tree answered, "Old tree roots are the best place to lean and rest on." "Come, come sit down with me and rest. " The boy sat down and the tree was glad and smiled with tears.

This tree is the father. When we were young, we loved to play with him. When we grew up, we left him only to come to him when we needed something or we were in trouble. Throughout all the changing scenes of life, fathers do play a role to presumptuous children who think that fathers have nothing else to offer. Being presumptuous and short-sighted, these sons say, "My father's time is past. He is irrelevant to the times." But time, the weather, the elements and the realities of life will reveal to all of such sons that a father is forever a father!

### The Short-sighted Son Sees His Father as Outmoded

Many fathers are viewed as outmoded or irrelevant, much like good food that has an expiration date. A father, however, never becomes irrelevant. Fathers become even more relevant as time goes by. If your mind is open and you have a humble spirit you will recognize that a father is never outmoded or irrelevant.

*It is of the Lord's mercies that we are not consumed, because his compassions fail not. THEY ARE NEW EVERY MORNING: great is thy faithfulness.* LAMENTATIONS 3:22-23

Many of the blessings spoken in the Bible came from fathers in the very last hours of their lives. Those words spoken by old departing fathers have affected generations of people. Isaac prophesied over his children in his last days. Obviously, he had not become irrelevant to the lives of his children. Had he been irrelevant, what he said would not have come to pass.

## The Short-sighted Son Sees Only "The Things" He Can Get From His Father

When short-sighted, a son has a very limited understanding of what he will receive from his father. The prodigal son walked away from his father after asking for his "portion." Some children see the relationship with their fathers in terms of money or items that they can receive. As a result, they do not benefit from the true blessing of the father. For instance, children may look at their parents only as someone who will pay their school fees. Beyond this, they do not expect or want anything else from them. Other children, like the boy in this story, see parents primarily as the people who will give them an inheritance – the only worthwhile thing they can receive from their father. Some children even hope their parents will die soon, so they can acquire what their parents have.

Because of this short-sightedness, they lose out on the many intangible, but even more powerful blessings that a father can bring to a son's life.

## The Short-sighted Son Cannot See the Invisible, Non-tangible Influence and Contributions a Father's Presence Makes

Many are the invisible and non-tangible things a father brings into a child's life. How myopic can you be to think that your father's usefulness is limited to buying stuff and paying your school fees? *How truly myopic the prodigal son was when he thought his father's usefulness was limited to a portion of inheritance!*

What did he do with the portion of inheritance? Did he prosper with the portion of inheritance? Was he successful with a portion of inheritance? Did his life change even though he had that portion of inheritance? Certainly not! He became poorer and lost everything even though he had gone away with a complete portion of inheritance.

Obviously there were certain unseen and perhaps intangible things that his father possessed that he had not yet received. Indeed he had a portion of the inheritance, but he had not received the wisdom and maturity his father had to give. Without the accompanying wisdom, prudence and understanding a father gives, his money often amounts to nothing. A father provides stability, wisdom, direction, influence, guidance, security, safety and a host of other intangible blessings.

## The Short-sighted Son Quickly Thinks He Has Received All He Could Ever Receive From His Father

A short-sighted son disconnects from the umbilical cord long before he should have. He is quick to conclude that he has received everything and all the teachings the father has to offer. I have met many people who say to themselves, "I know what he teaches. I know what he has to say. I know what he does."

You may ask, "How do I know?" It is the easiest thing in the world to perceive when you are with people who think they know you and know all about you. Remember, this is what the devil said to Jesus: "I know thee, who thou art." It is this line of thinking that evil spirits latch onto and inspire sons to abandon their fathers, or to leave the house unceremoniously.

I often notice pastors who think they know all about me. I smile to myself as they walk away with a portion they think they have received only to waste it and it amounts to nothing. Sometimes a father gives a portion away but keeps some things that he intends to give at the very end. Isaac gave things to his sons at the very end of his life that he did not bother to give earlier. How immature and narrow-minded you show yourself to be when you walk away thinking you have every bit of knowledge and wisdom your father has to offer!

**The Karate Master**

There was once a karate master who was the champion of all the provinces. He was well versed in a hundred punches, kicking, knee and elbow strikes. He was also an expert in one hundred open-hand techniques such as knife hands. He also knew a hundred grappling locks, restraints and throws. Above all, he had ten vital-point strikes that were his winning moves. This came to a total of three hundred and ten important karate moves. The master took a special liking to one of his pupils to whom he taught a total of three hundred and nine tricks. Somehow, he never got around to teaching him the last vital move.

As the months went by the pupil became so good at karate that he boasted that he could beat everyone including his master. Indeed, he said it was only out of respect for his age and gratitude for what he had been taught that he would not humiliate his master. In time the master heard about his pupil's bragging and decided to teach his disciple a lesson. He offered himself for a match with his pupil and crowds gathered to watch the only young man who could defeat the master.

When the gong sounded, the disciple rushed at his master only to be confronted with the unfamiliar three hundred and tenth-karate strike. The master lifted his former pupil above his head and flung him headlong to the ground amidst loud cheers from the audience. Later, when asked how he was able to defeat such a strong young man the master confessed that he had reserved the three hundred and tenth secret technique for himself, just in case it was needed for such an event.

There are many sons and disciples who think they have learned everything that there is to learn, only to discover to their dismay that there was much more that they could have learned.

## CHAPTER 18

# True Sons and Their Rewards

One day, a couple sat before me at the counselling table. The lady said to me, "Oh Bishop, I am your daughter." But I corrected her and said, "You are not my daughter, you are just a church member." She looked hurt, but I continued, "You are a very nice church member who is always smiling around and encouraging us but that doesn't make you a daughter. You are a VNP but you are not a daughter."

There are five types of church members: very nice people (VNPs), very encouraging people (VEPs), very important people (VIPs), very significant people (VSPs) and very dangerous people (VDPs). I went on to explain:

"When you see my children running around in the church, how do you know that they are my children?" She didn't answer so I answered myself, "They look like me. Can't you see that my children look like me?" She nodded. Then I asked her, "What similarity is there between you and me? You are not involved in the work of ministry. You are not a shepherd. You do nothing to help, and you do nothing in the church. You are a very nice person but not a daughter!"

She finally understood the point I was making. Just being around and being nice does not make you a son or a daughter. On that day, there were many children playing around after church, but only two of them were my sons. Being around doesn't make you a son. So what are the things that make you a son?

There are certain things that make you a son or a daughter, and that is what I will discuss in this chapter.

## Marks of a True Son and Daughter

## A Son or Daughter Resembles Their Father

> *Jesus saith unto him, Have I been so long time with you, and yet hast thou not known me, Philip? HE THAT HATH SEEN ME HATH SEEN THE FATHER…* John 14:9

When you see my sons and daughters in the ministry, you will find that they have some resemblance to me. The similarities between sons and fathers are the tell tale signs of the link between the fathers and the sons.

My biological children look like me and even have my colour. Spiritually, and in the ministry, there are many similarities between my sons and daughters in the Lord and myself. Jesus said, "He that has seen me has seen the Father." The reason why I don't have to run around all the different churches preaching is because my sons and daughters are ministering powerfully. If you have seen the son, then you have seen the father.

A son is not a clone or a photocopy of his father. But he has very important and essential traits that he received from his father. Every son has his father's genes, blood type and DNA. There are some sons who take after their fathers so closely that they look very much like them. On the other hand, there are sons who have very few similarities to their fathers even though they are real sons.

## A Son or Daughter Is Forever

> *And the servant abideth not in the house forever: but the Son*

*abideth ever.* JOHN 8:35

Real sons and daughters will always belong to your house. No matter what your natural child does, he always belongs to your house. He may have different beliefs, but he belongs to your family. In his heart, he knows where he belongs. He knows who brought him up and how he came to be what he is. A true son will seldom rise up against his own father.

*They went out from us, but they were not of us; for if they had been of us, they would no doubt have continued with us: but they went out, that they might be made manifest that they were not all of us.* 1 JOHN 2:19

## Sons and Daughters Believe in Their Fathers and Trust Them for Everything

*...Our Father which art in heaven, Hallowed be thy name. Thy kingdom come. Thy will be done in earth, as it is in heaven, Give us this day our daily bread.*

*And forgive us our debts, as we forgive our debtors. And lead us not into temptation, but deliver us from evil...*
MATTHEW 6:9-13

Real sons are filled with lots of trust. Most work places are filled with untrusting people. The junior staffs do not trust their manager. The managers do not trust their subordinates.

But in a family, the children usually trust their father absolutely. It may have happened, but I have never heard of children going on strike or demonstrating against their parents. The more we trust God, the more of his blessings we experience. Differences between children of the same family usually stem from the different levels of trust they have for their father.

In the ministry, I notice the same thing. More of God's blessings and anointing flow through me to sons and daughters who are more trusting. Some sons and daughters are wary and suspicious. Others are more trusting and filled with faith. The trusting children always get more of their father's blessings. These differences come from the different extents to which they trust their fathers and what their fathers say.

> *If ye then, being evil, know how to give good gifts unto your children...* LUKE 11:13

Jesus believed in His Father's ability. He believed that His Father was powerful. He understood the power of His Father. His very last words on the cross were to entrust Himself into His Father's care: "Father, into thine hands I commend my spirit." With those words He plucked his soul out of the jaws of death and placed it into the hands of His Father.

> *And when Jesus had cried with a loud voice, he said, Father, into thy hands I commend my spirit: and having said thus, he gave up the ghost.* LUKE 23:46

He believed in his Father and even when the terrors of death were closing in on Him, He knew who had the power to rescue Him. That is the power of a father, which Jesus respected. Is it not amazing that His very last words on earth shed such light on the Son's belief in His Father? Stupendous!

## A Son Honors His Father

> *A son honoreth his father, and a servant his master: if then I be a father, where is mine honor...?* MALACHI 1:6

Don't expect honor from servants or employees. You can only expect lip service and fake smiles from employees. You can expect honor from a real son. In the Old Testament, priests were essentially a group of children who ministered alongside their father.

One megachurch pastor said to me, "I have had many bad experiences by appointing pastors from other churches and Bible schools. Now I only have my own spiritual sons and daughters working with me in the ministry." That is the way it should be! Your true sons and daughters will only bring you honor. Apart from a few prodigal sons, most sons and daughters bring honor and joy to their father.

God has often led me to honor people who have been fathers to me. I have tried to honor them in private and in public. I have honored them with my words and with my substance.

True sons and daughters honor their father with their substance. It is a shame for your father or mother to struggle financially when you could help them. Do you want your parents to beg you for money? That is not honoring your father! That is humiliating to him.

Even when your father and mother do not need anything, you must honor them with your substance because that is what the Bible teaches.

> *A son honoreth his father, and a servant his master: IF THEN I BE A FATHER, WHERE IS MINE HONOR? and if I be a master, where is my fear? saith the LORD of hosts unto you, O priests, that despise my name. And ye say, Wherein have we despised thy name? Ye offer polluted bread upon mine altar; and ye say, Wherein have we polluted thee? In that ye say, The table of the LORD is contemptible. And if ye offer the blind for sacrifice, is it not evil? and if ye offer the lame and sick, is it not evil? offer it now unto thy governor; will he be pleased with thee, or accept thy person? saith the LORD of hosts.* MALACHI 1:6-8

## Sons and Daughters Obey Their Fathers

> *Children, obey your parents in the Lord: for this is right. Honor thy father and mother; (which is the first commandment with promise ;) That it may be well with thee, and thou mayest live long on the earth.* EPHESIANS 6:1-3

Lots of rebellious people love to call themselves sons and daughters. But, they are no more a son or daughter than I am an astronaut. True sons obey their fathers! Do not try to exert authority over people who are not your true sons or daughters in the ministry. They will only disobey you because they are not your true sons and daughters. Your real sons and daughters will obey you. When I sense that someone is not a son or daughter, I am very limited in what I tell the person to do. It is only true sons and daughters who obey.

## Sons and Daughters Do What They See Their Fathers Do

> *...The Son can do nothing of himself, but what he seeth the Father do: for what things soever he doeth, these also doeth the Son likewise.* JOHN 5:19B

A true son looks at what his father does. He is interested in what his father is doing and thinks that his father knows the right way. This is what Jesus did. He healed only those He saw His Father healing and He preached only when He saw His Father preaching.

Sons are rarely wiser than their fathers. Why didn't Jesus heal the whole multitude by the pool of Bethesda? He healed one man and left the rest untouched. It is like going into a hospital and healing only one person. It may not make sense to you, but that is what the Father did. Jesus was content to do what He saw His Father doing.

I have sons and daughters in the ministry who flourish when they do what they see me doing. They preach what I preach and they teach what I teach. They see me healing the sick and they start to heal the sick. They do not do this because they are mindless clones; *they are simply good sons and good daughters!* Good sons are fast followers.

Of course, any human father (like me) is imperfect and his life will never be the perfect example of things to follow. Our ultimate example is Christ! But God gives fathers on this earth so that we have practical examples to follow.

## Sons Carry the Words of Their Fathers

Another sign of a true son is that he carries the words of his father. He hears the words of his father often and he repeats them whenever he can.

Sometimes you hear him repeating the words of his father in conversation and sometimes he preaches what his father has preached. As Jesus said, "He that hath seen me hath seen the Father." People ask the sons, "How do you know all these things? Where did you get this wisdom from?" Simply put, they are repeating the words of their fathers.

> *When I was a son to my father, Tender and the only son in the sight of my mother, then he taught me and said to me, "Let your heart hold fast my words; Keep my commandments and live;"*
> PROVERBS 4:3-4 (NASB)

## Three Rewards for Honoring Fathers

> *Children, obey your parents in the Lord: for this is right. Honor thy father and mother; which is the first commandment with promise; THAT IT MAY BE WELL WITH THEE, AND THOU MAYEST LIVE LONG ON THE EARTH.*
> EPHESIANS 6:1-3

## The First Reward: That it May Be Well With You

When it is well with you, you will:

A. Be successful
B. Overcome
C. Thrive
D. Flower
E. Multiply
F. Recover
G. Hit it big
H. Prosper
I. Develop
J. Increase
K. Win

L. Get ahead
M. Do well
N. Bear fruit
O. Expand

One of the highest blessings of honoring one's father and mother is that it may be well with you. Who would not like it to be well with him or her? However, it will never be well with you if you are disobedient to your father! The great blessing for sons is hidden in their obedience to their fathers.

There is something I have noticed in large families with many children. The sons or daughters who are very obedient to their parents turn out differently from those who are rebellious, independent and resistant. It is a pattern you will discover for yourself. One pastor told me how she had noticed this phenomenon. She described how some of her father's children had constantly resisted their father's advice. "It is not easy for them today," she said. "Marriage is not easy. And financially, it is very difficult for them." She continued, "I can see a clear difference between those of us who obeyed and those who rebelled."

## The Difference Is Clear

Another pastor said to me, "I have a big family with many brothers and sisters but the difference is clear." He described how his father was cared for by one of his daughters.

He said to me, "This sister of mine cared for my father all the time. She did what he wanted and he was always pleased with her." "In fact," he continued, "*my father died in her arms. She was nursing him when he died. Even my mother was not around when he died but she was there.*"

Today, her life is very different from some of her brothers and sisters. He began to describe horrific conditions of the cancer and poverty which had struck some of his other brothers and sisters. He mused, "There is certainly a difference between children who love and honor their parents and those who don't."

One day, a father went shopping with his two sons. As they walked through the department store buying clothes, the father suggested to his sons, "Take this pair of trousers, it will suit you, it is nice." But there was a clear difference in the response of the sons to their father's suggestions. One of them constantly had a different opinion. He didn't like what his father liked. He always wanted something different. He even became grumpy and angry because he couldn't have some things. The reaction of the other son, however, was very different. He would say, "Whatever you choose for me is okay. I like what you like for me. *I want what you want for me.*"

You see, these two attitudes can grow up and result in two different outcomes. The highest kind of blessing is that it may be well with you. It will be well with daughters who trust and obey their fathers! It will be well with sons who trust and obey their fathers. This principle applies to all kinds of fathers whether natural or spiritual.

Be a son who wants what his father wants for him. Be a son who likes what his father likes. Christianity is based on this principle -- the principle of submitting your will to the will of your father. The principle of *accepting the father's will* instead of your own will.

Do not be self-willed. Be subject to your father's will. It is safer and easier to say, "Father, into thine hands do I commit my life." Let's follow Jesus; He is the best example for us all.

## The Second Reward: That You May Live Long

When you honor your father you will:

A. Overcome diseases that shorten life

B. Survive many crises

C. Continue in spite of danger

D. Endure many difficulties

E. Last a long time

F. Stay alive when people predict your death

G. Live to tell the tale

H. Be able to persist in the ministry

I. Prolong your life

J. Stay afloat

K. Make a comeback
L. Outlast others
M. Outlive others
N. Outwear others
O. Pull through
P. Tough it out
Q. Come through
R. Go all the way
S. 'Never say die'
T. Be timeless

One of the sure ways to shorten your life is to dishonor your father and mother. Look around carefully and you will find this to be practically true. *In the ministry, your longevity is also determined by your relationship with your spiritual leaders.* Longevity speaks of how long you last in the ministry. You will always meet people ahead of you. It is important to honor these people as leaders. Even when you have a different ministry, you must respect pastors and spiritual leaders for who they are.

Two biblical examples of long-lasting ministries are those of Jesus and David. Jesus' ministry has spanned thousands of years and is getting stronger. The ministry of King David is still being felt through the Psalms he wrote and the life he led. If you want to survive and persist through the years, learn this principle now!

## The Third Reward: Receiving an Inheritance

> *The eyes of your understanding being enlightened; that ye may know what is the hope of his calling, and what the riches of the glory of his inheritance in the saints.* EPHESIANS 1:18

What is your "spiritual inheritance?" A spiritual inheritance is something that passes from fathers to sons. Only when you receive a man of God in your life as a father, do you receive the benefit of the inheritance. An inheritance will only flow from the fathers to their sons and daughters.

You will notice from the story of Elisha that he had an earthly father called Shaphat.

> *...Here is Elisha the son of Shaphat...* 2 KINGS 3:11

However, at the time Elijah was being taken away, Elisha referred to Elijah as his father. He did this effortlessly and naturally.

> *And Elisha saw it, and he cried, My father, my father...*
> 2 KINGS 2:12

Why is it important to receive your man of God as a father? Because fathers leave behind an inheritance for their children. People usually do not leave an inheritance for servants, employees, friends and colleagues. *The inheritance is meant for the children!* A person with an inheritance is very different from someone without one. A person with a father receives guidance and direction for his life. A fatherless person has a life full of struggles.

I never worked while I was in the university. My father provided for me fully until I became a doctor. The money he gave me each month as a student was more than my salary when I became a doctor. My father bought me a brand new car when I was in the fifth year of medical school. I was really blessed to have a good father looking after me. *My life as a student was "struggle-free" because I had a father!* However, the same cannot be said for many people.

I have met countless people who did not receive such guidance for their lives. They threw away their talents and became non-entities because there was no father to guide them. I know many people who do not even know their fathers. The situation is even worse for orphans! Struggles abound for orphans. The future of an orphan is very uncertain.

It is the same in ministry. When you have no one to influence you in the right way, your ministry is full of struggles. Although I have had different fathers in ministry, there were times I was fatherless as far as developing into a pastor was concerned. I have had fathers in ministry from afar. I have gone through various struggles because I did not receive support from nearby fathers. Many of the struggles and frustrations I experienced in ministry were because I had no one to help me. In fact, people who should have been fathers to me when I was beginning my church were more of outright enemies. They opposed my cause and fought against me.

*Inheritance flows naturally from a father to his children.* In the ministry, a spiritual inheritance flows naturally from the fathers to the sons. When my father died, his will was read in Court. He left his properties to his children. Although he had many employees and friends, he didn't will anything to them. Everything went to his children.

Dear friend, that is the reality of life. The inheritance always goes to children and not to colleagues and friends. Similarly, a spiritual inheritance of anointing and gifts passes naturally from fathers to sons. It does not pass from father to equals, colleagues and friends. It does not even pass from father to servants. It passes from *fathers to sons.*

### Hello "Boss"

I used to have a junior pastor who preferred to call me "boss." I always felt uneasy when he called me "boss," but I didn't know why. You see, when someone calls you "boss," it means that he sees himself more as a hired hand. A few years later, this pastor departed under unpleasant circumstances. Then I realized why I had felt uneasy. A servant or an employee does not stay around forever. He's only there for a while and will leave when it suits him.

> *And the servant abideth not in the house for ever: but the Son abideth ever.* JOHN 8:35

If you have a relationship with a man of God, which becomes a father/son relationship, you can expect a spiritual inheritance of anointing to flow effortlessly from him to you.

## A Final Exhortation to Practice the Art of the Follower

God wants our obedience to Him. He wants us to follow after Him with all our heart. Our ardent and faithful following -- the practice of all we have already discussed in this book -- gain for us sonship and eternal salvation. The most fulfilling reward for our obedience, however, comes when it is motivated by a profoundly simple heart response to God's great grace, mercy and love bestowed on us. It is to love Him back, to please Him and to draw closer to Him that we practice the art of the follower!

This is the uniqueness of Christ's glorious gospel. This truly is "good news." Moralistic religion works on the principle, "I obey, therefore God accepts me." The gospel works on the principle, "I am accepted by God through Jesus Christ, therefore I obey; I follow." These are two radically different, even opposite, dynamics. Yet both sets of people are followers. They sit in church together, both pray, both obey the Ten Commandments, but for radically different reasons which produce radically different results--different kinds of spiritual character. One typically yields anger, joyless compliance, superiority, insecurity and a condemning spirit. The other slowly but inevitably produces contentment, joy, humility, poise and a forgiving spirit.

Whether in your human family or your spiritual family, be careful which motive for being a Christ follower you are encouraging. Be certain that God's grace abounds in your heart and your practice. Recognize over and over that what Christ did for you on the cross was intended to drain you of all self-righteousness and insecurity. Have the grateful and repentant spirit of the younger son. Seek to never again display the spirit of the elder brother, which is to presume that even your active obedience can add anything at all to why you are saved and worthy of heaven.

It is my prayer that from this day forth, you will more consistently bask moment by moment in God's marvellous grace and more willingly trust Him with all your heart to faithfully follow our Saviour and those leaders you know who also are truly following Him.

# Bishop Dag Heward-Mills: Shining Radiant Arcs of Light World-wide

He has been called a "faithful servant," an "inspiration to Christianity" and a "ray of hope and healing" to the lost and hurting around the world. Many have compared his passion for sharing the Gospel to the brilliant beam of a lighthouse, "his eyes burning with a vision" that illumines the Way for millions of seekers across the globe.

Indeed, over the past 20 years, evangelist, pastor and author Dag Heward-Mills has impacted millions through a multi-faceted world-wide ministry—one that shines with many amazing, bold arcs of light. An array of soul-winning projects, all of which he leads, directs or has written, are woven together to create a powerful force for Christ. And today they continue to gain brilliance and momentum.

These bright, evangelistic embers can be traced back to a time decades ago. Born in the UK to a Ghanaian lawyer and Swiss mother and growing up in the West African coastal country of Ghana, Dag gave his life to the Lord as a teenager. Soon after, while completing a seven-year training program at the University of Ghana Medical School, he felt God anointing him to teach and, testifying to God's fervent call on his life, began holding meetings in a campus classroom. As attendance swelled, meetings were moved to larger and larger rooms—and thus the first Lighthouse Chapel was born. Meanwhile, Dag earned his medical degree in 1989 and was ordained into the ministry in London the following year. Six years later, in 1996, the International Ministerial Council of Great Britain consecrated him as bishop.

Through all these occurrences, one of many sweeps of light began to intensely shine. As more churches were planted under Dag's leadership as presiding bishop, Lighthouse Chapel International (LCI) grew into a world-wide denomination with almost 1300 churches spreading across every continent in 60 countries, including 63 churches in the United States. Back in Accra, Ghana (LCI's home base), Bishop Heward-Mills commissioned in 2006 the construction of one of the largest church complexes in Africa—called the Qodesh (the Hebrew word for consecrated, dedicated or Holy Hill)—where attendance today often overflows its capacity.

Yet another gleaming glint of light appeared in 2004 when Dag held an evangelistic event, sparking the much-acclaimed Healing Jesus Crusades across Africa and other third-world countries. Today, this ministry seems to glow with God's blessing. Picture massive crowds gathering, listening and responding to the truth of God's Word, with thousands committing their lives to Christ and others receiving healing in His name. While the first crusade drew just over 600 attendees, each gathering now attracts up to five hundred thousand at each event.

To follow up each crusade, faith-building books and pamphlets written by Bishop Heward-Mills are freely "seeded" to help disciple and lead throngs of new believers to a closer walk with Christ. In fact, the Bishop is now known as a prolific author, with more than 73 titles to date, including 30 international bestsellers and many new releases anticipated in the coming months (including the much-acclaimed 5-book series *Loyalty and Disloyalty*). These books, including bestseller *The Art of the Follower* and many others, help pastors build stronger churches and motivate readers to effectively bolster their ministries, families and marriages.

Still other lights sparkle in multiple arenas—inspiring the next generation to ministry, healing the sick and rescuing orphans from lives of pain and abuse. In 1995, the Bishop established the Lighthouse Christian Mission Schools and, in 1997, added the Anagkazo Bible and Ministry Training Center. In 2006, he established three more rays of hope: the Lighthouse Mission Hospital, the Healing Jesus Medical Missions and the Lighthouse Christian Orphanage. Partnering with other ministries, Dag and his dedicated team are helping communities around the globe.

The list continues. He has held multiple conferences to equip church leaders, serves on the board of Church Growth International and produces radio and TV programs, DVD's and CD's, all to share the Gospel world-wide. He has also teamed up with his wife, Adelaide, to speak to crowds across Africa on the importance of a strong, faith-filled marriage and its vital role in the life of a Christian.

The blessed parents of four wonderful children—David, Joshua, Daniella and Paula—Dag and Adelaide reside in Accra, Ghana, where their passion for outreach continues to radiantly shine. Indeed, the Bishop and his ministry team have set robust goals, which include "to build 25,000 churches in 150 countries," "to continue to fight fiercely and relentlessly in all battles for the advancement of the churches and the Gospel" and "to produce passionate Christians who work for God."

Perhaps a final goal, in its simplicity, proves the most telling: "to go to Heaven and hear Jesus say, 'Well done, good and faithful servant.'" Looking back, Bishop Dag Heward-Mills may indeed see many arcs of light all intertwined—a unified beam cutting through the darkness as millions are enlightened with the hope of the Gospel. Until then, the "faithful servant" stands in the lighthouse, shining the Way.

www.daghewardmills.org